The New Science
of Politics

Posterity may know we have not loosely through silence permitted things to pass away as in a dream.

RICHARD HOOKER

The New Science of Politics

An Introduction

ERIC VOEGELIN

With a new Foreword by
Dante Germino

THE UNIVERSITY OF CHICAGO PRESS

CHICAGO & LONDON

CHARLES R. WALGREEN FOUNDATION LECTURES

THE UNIVERSITY OF CHICAGO PRESS, CHICAGO 60637
THE UNIVERSITY OF CHICAGO PRESS, LTD., London

© 1952, 1987 by The University of Chicago
All rights reserved. Published 1952
Midway Reprint edition 1983. Paperback edition 1987
Printed in the United States of America

ISBN 0–226–86114–7
LCN 52–13531

FOREWORD, 1987

✿

THIRTY-FIVE years ago, few could have predicted that *The New Science of Politics* would be a best-seller by political theory standards. Compressed within the Draconian economy of the six Walgreen lectures is a complete theory of man, society, and history, presented at the most profound intellectual level. Interlarded with tongue-twisting technical terms derived mostly from classical Greek, the argument ranges over topics ordinarily discussed only among small circles of scholars.

It was Eric Voegelin's great gift, however, to be able to draw out the contemporary political relevance of such seemingly arcane subjects as the Behistun Inscription, the Mongol Orders of Submission, and the controversy over the altar to the goddess Victoria in the Roman Forum. Milking the specialized monographic literature dry of its implications for a theory of order and history, Voegelin writes in a manner that grips the attention of any serious reader.

The book's argument can best be understood under Voegelin's original title: *Truth and Representation*. With remarkable erudition and economy of expression, Voegelin discusses in turn what he calls the "cosmological," "anthropological," and "soteriological" symbolizations of truth, and then contrasts all of them with "gnosticism." Cosmological symbols tend to portray a given society's institutions as a reflection of the order observable in the visible heavens. Anthropological symbols reflect the discovery of the psyche and its attempts at attunement with an invisible order of right judgment beyond the visible order of the heavens. Soteriological symbols indicate the experience of human beings who open their psyches to the unveiling of the unseen measure in time by a God who reaches out to man through grace. Myth, philosophy, and revelation are the three symbolic forms in which the cosmological, anthropological, and soteriological experiences find assuaging expression.

Gnosticism is a symbolic form at least as old as the Christian Era itself; it arose out of the fragile nature of earthly existence, which leaves many people thirsting for a certain and immediate deliverance from so hazardous a condition. The Gnostic creed-movement gives its followers a sense of superiority over the uninitiated, and its sage typically believes that he has become one with the godhead and has achieved liberation from the world of ordinary human beings.

While early Gnosticism tended to be politically quietistic, it later became revolutionary and destructive in the West. This was a result of the coincidence of the revival of ancient Gnosticism with the remarkable expansion of power resulting from the growth of urban centers and increased trade. Joachim of Fiore, a twelfth-century Calabrian monk who founded a new religious order, gave Western civilization the three-stage periodization of history which made possible the conceptualization of modernity itself. Joachim's division of history into the Ages of Father, Son, and Holy Ghost was the forerunner of Flavio Biondo's periodization of history into ancient, medieval, and modern eras, and of the Third Realm constructions in Condorcet, Comte, Marx, Lenin, and Hitler.

The paradox of modernity is that it is an age that advances and declines at the same time. On the one hand, the centuries since the Renaissance and Reformation have brought forth civil and international wars of unprecedented destructiveness. Many of these wars were without rational cause and waged with objectives impossible to attain. The public life of modern societies has become increasing materialistic and has fostered widespread alienation. The result has been a growing body of literature on the "decline" of the West. On the other hand, those who hail the modern era as one of stupendous progress also have a case. Prodigious advances in the sciences and technology have led to an unprecedentedly high level of material comfort, health, literacy, and philanthropy.

The "thorny question" of how a civilization can simultaneously advance and decline may be at least partially answered by analyzing modern Gnosticism. In four pages (129–32) Voegelin magisterially summarizes the book's argument, maintaining that modern Gnosticism in its various forms— teleological, axiological, and activist—has overshadowed what is left of "the Mediterranean tradition." While the core of this tradition (Greek philosophy, Judaism, and Christianity) acknowledged the limitation of the human condition and the fundamental "uncertainty" of man's knowledge about the transcendent divine ground of all the exists, modern Gnosticism has been dedicated to the hubristic attempt to overcome the anxieties and uncertainties of human life by building a terrestrial paradise. However well-intentioned, even the "moderate" proponents of the "progressive" program bear a heavy responsibility for the disasters of modernity. However worthy specific projects for ameliorating human misery may be, they cannot serve as substitutes for the inner quest for transcendent reality that motivated Plato, Amos, and Paul. "The death of the spirit is the price of progress."

Voegelin is no Spengler, and his closing chaper is full of hope for the possibility of reversing the decline of modern civilization and recovering what in Greek philosophy, Judaism, and Christianity has been lost. The United States and Great Britain contain, for reasons he explains, the largest residue of the Mediterranean tradition, and together they are (or were in 1952) the world's strongest military powers. Voegelin's comments about the Soviet Union are strikingly free of alarm over the prospects of its expansion to world supremacy. With confidence in the future (although refusing to make Gnostic predictions of inevitability) he addresses to each reader an appeal to reorient priorities and accomplish the *periagoge* (or turning around) urged by the philosopher in the Parable of the Cave. With Plato, Voegelin could have written as his last words "We shall fare well."

Eric Voegelin's *New Science of Politics* stands out in bold relief from much of what has passed under the name of political science in recent decades. The opening chapter contains a scathing critique of positivist social science, of its zeal for collecting irrelevant facts and ignoring relevant ones, of its "taboo" on metaphysical questions, and of its appalling "theoretical illiteracy." The *New Science* is aptly titled, for Voegelin makes clear at the outset that "a return to the specific content" of premodern political theory is out of the question: "One cannot restore political science today through Platonism, Augustinianism, or Hegelianism" (p. 2).

Critics who label *The New Science of Politics* a "conservative" book might do well to read the work more carefully. Voegelin always rejected attempts to "position" him, and he was emphatic in counseling, "Don't be an Ism-ist!" In his combative way, he made apodictic pronouncements about contemporary issues or policies that may seem to some readers inconsistent with a philosophy of history centering on "uncertainty" in the sense of *Hebrews* 11:1: "Faith is the substance of things hoped for, the evidence of things unseen". Like any thinker, Voegelin wrote in the light cast by his experience. He watched the Austria where he spent most of his early life succumb to Nazism, and chose to escape across the border with only the clothes on his back rather than compromise with so evil a regime. These experiences left him with an understandable distrust of mass movements.

Some thoughtful readers, Alfred Schutz among them, were troubled by passages in *The New Science of Politics* wherein Voegelin seems to elevate Christianity above all other intellectual and spiritual orientations. Still others object to what appear at times to be blanket condemnations of liberalism. Usually a second reading of the argument will reveal a more nuanced aspect of the matter in question. For example, Voegelin distinguishes between "essential" Christianity as the experience of "uncertain truth" through faith in the sense of *Hebrews* 11, 1–3, and its deformation into dogmatic propositions detached from the experience itself. With reference to liberalism, readers should note the book's concluding paragraph in which Voegelin praises the "American and English democracies" as the most adequate contemporary representatives of the "truth of the soul."

Eric Voegelin himself was keenly aware that he had by no means said the last word on the subject of order and history. The subtitle of the book, *An Introduction,* clearly indicates that *The New Science of Politics* is an invitation to join the search for the recovery of our full humanity. As partners in the quest for reality, we can be grateful for the light he has cast upon the Way.

DANTE GERMINO
University of Virginia

FOREWORD

✿

DURING the last thirty years or more there have arisen among the students in the field of politics those who would challenge the traditional approach to government and politics—an approach stemming from the days of Aristotle. The statistical, the psychological, and the sociological bases of a political science have each had adherents. Propounders of the new theories have either pushed aside or rejected the consideration of any system of values in their theories of the scientific approach to politics. While this type of approach has widespread acceptance today, it is being vigorously challenged in many quarters, particularly on the very home ground of the scientific school, the University of Chicago. Professor Voegelin in the present work makes an interesting and challenging contribution to the scope and method of politics. His position as an outstanding scholar in the field of political theory is a guaranty of his thoroughness and objectivity in handling his topic.

Under the sponsorship of the Charles R. Walgreen Foundation these lectures were given at the University of Chicago during the Winter Quarter, 1951. The co-operation of the author and the University of Chicago enables the Foundation to publish this series.

JEROME G. KERWIN

Chairman, Charles R. Walgreen Foundation for the Study of American Institutions

ACKNOWLEDGMENTS

✣

ON OCCASION of this book I should like to express my gratitude to the John Simon Guggenheim Memorial Foundation for enabling me to bring the state of the problems up to date through studies in Europe in the summer of 1950. These studies were, furthermore, facilitated by a grant-in-aid from the Research Council of Louisiana State University.

My colleague, Professor Nelson E. Taylor, had the kindness to read the manuscript; I have gratefully availed myself of his advice in matters of style. My thanks for excellent secretarial help go to Miss Josephine Scurria. The Viking Press has kindly permitted the quotation of passages from a book published by it.

This book has grown from six lectures on "Truth and Representation" given in 1951 under the auspices of the Charles R. Walgreen Foundation. It is a pleasant opportunity to extend my thanks again to the Foundation as well as to its distinguished chairman, Professor Jerome G. Kerwin.

BATON ROUGE, LOUISIANA

ERIC VOEGELIN

TABLE OF CONTENTS

✿

INTRODUCTION

✿

1

THE existence of man in political society is historical existence; and a theory of politics, if it penetrates to principles, must at the same time be a theory of history. The following lectures on the central problem of a theory of politics, on representation, will, therefore, carry the inquiry beyond a description of the conventionally so-called representative institutions into the nature of representation as the form by which a political society gains existence for action in history. Moreover, the analysis will not stop at this point but will proceed to an exploration of the symbols by which political societies interpret themselves as representatives of a transcendent truth. And the manifold of such symbols, finally, will not form a flat catalogue but prove amenable to theoretization as an intelligible succession of phases in a historical process. An inquiry concerning representation, if its theoretical implications are unfolded consistently, will in fact become a philosophy of history.

To pursue a theoretical problem to the point where the principles of politics meet with the principles of a philosophy of history is not customary today. Nevertheless, the procedure cannot be considered an innovation in political science; it will rather appear as a restoration, if it be remembered that the two fields which today are cultivated separately were inseparably united when political science was founded by Plato. This integral theory of politics was born from the crisis of Hellenic society. In an hour of crisis, when the order of a society flounders and disintegrates, the fundamental problems of political existence in history are more apt to come into view than in periods of comparative stability. Ever since, one may say, the contraction of political science to a description of existing institutions and the apology of their principles, that is, the degradation of political science to a handmaid of the powers that be, has been typical for stable situations, while its expansion to its full grandeur as the science of human existence in society and history, as well as of the principles of order in general, has been typical for the great epochs of a revolutionary and critical nature. On the largest scale of Western history three such epochs occurred. The foundation of political science through Plato and Aristotle marked the Hellenic crisis; St. Augustine's *Civitas Dei* marked the crisis of Rome and Christianity; and Hegel's philosophy of law and history marked the first major earthquake of the Western crisis. These are only the great epochs and the great restorations; the millennial periods between them are marked by minor epochs and secondary restorations; for the modern period, in particular, one should remember the great attempt of Bodin in the crisis of the sixteenth century.

By restoration of political science is meant a return to the consciousness of principles, not perhaps a return to the specific content of an earlier attempt. One cannot restore political science today through Platonism, Augustinianism, or Hegelianism. Much can be learned, to be sure, from the earlier philosophers concerning the range of problems, as well as concerning their theoretical treatment; but the very historicity of human existence, that is, the unfolding of the typical in meaningful concreteness, precludes a valid reformulation of principles through return to a former concreteness. Hence, political science cannot be restored to the dignity of a theoretical science in the strict sense by means of a literary renaissance of philosophical achievements of the past; the principles must be regained by a work of theoretization which starts from the concrete, historical situation of the age, taking into account the full amplitude of our empirical knowledge.

Formulated in such terms, the task looks formidable under any circumstances; and it may look hopeless in view of the enormous amounts of material which the empirical sciences of society and history put at our disposition today. In fact, however, this impression is deceptive. While the difficulties should by no means be underrated, the task begins to become feasible in our time because of the preparatory work that has been done during the last half-century. For two generations, now, the sciences of man and society are engaged in a process of re-theoretization. The new development, slow at first, gained momentum after the first World War; and today it is moving at a breathtaking speed. The task is approaching feasibility because, to a considerable extent, it is accomplished through convergent theoretization of the relevant materials in monographic studies. The title for these lectures on representation, *The New Science of Politics*, indicates the intention of introducing the reader to a development of political science which as yet is practically unknown to the general public as well as of showing that the monographic exploration of problems has reached the point where the application of results to a basic theoretical problem in politics can at least be attempted.

2

The movement toward retheoretization is not too well known, either in its range or in its accomplishments. And this is not the occasion for a description which, in order to be adequate, would have to run to considerable length. Nevertheless, a few indications must be given concerning its causes and intentions in order to answer some of the questions that inevitably will occur to the reader of the following lectures.

A restoration of political science to its principles implies that the restorative work is necessary because the conscious-

ness of principles is lost. The movement toward retheoretization must be understood, indeed, as a recovery from the destruction of science which characterized the positivistic era in
the second half of the nineteenth century. The destruction
worked by positivism is the consequence of two fundamental
assumptions. In the first place, the splendid unfolding of the
natural sciences was co-responsible with other factors for the
assumption that the methods used in the mathematizing sciences of the external world were possessed of some inherent
virtue and that all other sciences would achieve comparable
success if they followed the example and accepted these methods as their model. This belief by itself was a harmless idio-
syncrasy that would have died out when the enthusiastic ad-
mirers of the model method set to work in their own science
and did not achieve the expected successes. It became dangerous because it combined with the second assumption that the
methods of the natural sciences were a criterion for theoretical
relevance in general. From the combination of the two assumptions followed the well-known series of assertions that a
study of reality could qualify as scientific only if it used the
methods of the natural sciences, that problems couched in
other terms were illusionary problems, that in particular metaphysical questions which do not admit of answers by the
methods of the sciences of phenomena should not be asked,
that realms of being which are not accessible to exploration
by the model methods were irrelevant, and, in the extreme,
that such realms of being did not exist.

The second assumption is the real source of danger. It is the
key to the understanding of positivistic destructiveness, and it
has by far not received the attention which it deserves. For
this second assumption subordinates theoretical relevance to
method and thereby perverts the meaning of science. Science
is a search for truth concerning the nature of the various
realms of being. Relevant in science is whatever contributes to

the success of this search. Facts are relevant in so far as their knowledge contributes to the study of essence, while methods are adequate in so far as they can be effectively used as a means for this end. Different objects require different methods. A political scientist who tries to understand the meaning of Plato's *Republic* will not have much use for mathematics; a biologist who studies a cell structure will not have much use for methods of classical philology and principles of hermeneutics. This may sound trivial, but disregard for elementary verities happens to be one of the characteristics of the positivistic attitude; and hence it becomes necessary to elaborate the obvious. It is perhaps a consolation to remember that such disregard is a perennial problem in the history of science, for even Aristotle had to remind certain pests of his time that an "educated man" will not expect exactness of the mathematical type in a treatise on politics.

If the adequacy of a method is not measured by its usefulness to the purpose of science, if on the contrary the use of a method is made the criterion of science, then the meaning of science as a truthful account of the structure of reality, as the theoretical orientation of man in his world, and as the great instrument for man's understanding of his own position in the universe is lost. Science starts from the prescientific existence of man, from his participation in the world with his body, soul, intellect, and spirit, from his primary grip on all the realms of being that is assured to him because his own nature is their epitome. And from this primary cognitive participation, turgid with passion, rises the arduous way, the *methodos*, toward the dispassionate gaze on the order of being in the theoretical attitude. The question whether in the concrete case the way was the right one, however, can be decided only by looking back from the end to the beginning. If the method has brought to essential clarity the dimly seen, then it was adequate; if it has failed to do so, or even if it has brought to essential clarity something in which concretely we were not interested, then it has proved inadequate. If, for instance, in our prescientific participation in the order of a society, in our prescientific experiences of right and wrong, of justice and injustice, we should feel the desire to penetrate to a theoretical understanding of the source of order and its validity, we may arrive in the course of our endeavors at the theory that the justice of human order depends on its participation in the Platonic Agathon, or the Aristotelian Nous, or the Stoic Logos, or the Thomistic *ratio aeterna*. For one reason or another, none of these theories may satisfy us completely; but we know that we are in search for an answer of this type. If, however, the way should lead us to the notion that social order is motivated by will to power and fear, we know that we have lost the essence of the problem somewhere in the course of our inquiry—however valuable the results may be in clarifying other essential aspects of social order. In looking back from the answer to the question, we know, therefore, that the methods of a psychology of motivations are not adequate for the exploration of the problem and that in this concrete case it would be better to rely on the methods of metaphysical speculation and theological symbolization.

The subordination of theoretical relevance to method perverts the meaning of science on principle. Perversion will result whatever method should happen to be chosen as the model method. Hence, the principle must be carefully distinguished from its special manifestation. Without the distinction it is hardly possible to understand the historical phenomenon of positivism in its nature and range; and probably, because the distinction is not made, an adequate study of this important phase of Western intellectual history is still a desideratum. While such an analysis cannot be supplied on this occasion, the rules that would have to be followed must be set forth in order to bring the variety of positivistic phenomena into view. The analysis would inevitably come to a wrong start if positivism were defined as the doctrine of this or that outstanding positivistic thinker—if it were defined, for instance, in terms of the system of Comte. The special form of the perversion would obscure the principle; and related phenomena could not be recognized as such, because on the level of doctrine the adherents of different model methods are apt to oppose each other. Hence, it would be advisable to start from the impression which the Newtonian system made on Western intellectuals like Voltaire; to treat this impact as an emotional center from which the principle of perversion, as well as the special form of the model of physics, can radiate independently or in combination; and to trace the effects whatever form they may assume. This procedure recommends itself especially because a transfer of methods of mathematical physics in any strict sense of the word to the social sciences has hardly ever been attempted, for the good reason that the attempt would be too patently doomed to failure. The idea of finding a "law" of social phenomena that functionally would correspond to the law of gravitation in Newtonian physics never went beyond the stage of wild talk in the Napoleonic era. By the time of Comte the idea had already simmered down to the "law" of the three phases, that is, to a piece of fallacious speculation on the meaning of history which interpreted itself as the discovery of an empirical law. Characteristic for the early diversification of the problem is the fate of the term *physique sociale*. Comte wanted to use it for his positivistic speculation but was thwarted in his intention because Quételet appropriated the term for his own statistical investigations; the area of social phenomena which are indeed amenable to quantification began to separate from the area where toying with an imitation of physics is a pastime for dilettantes in both sciences. Hence, if positivism should be construed in a strict sense as meaning the development of social science through the use of mathematizing methods, one might arrive at the conclusion that positivism has never existed; if, however, it is understood as the intention of making the social sciences "scientific" through the use of methods which as closely as possible resemble the methods employed in sciences of the external world, then the results of this intention (though not intended) will be rather variegated.

The theoretical issue of positivism as a historical phenomenon had to be stated with some care; the variety of manifestations themselves can be listed briefly, now that their uniting bond is understood. The use of method as the criterion of science abolishes theoretical relevance. As a consequence, all propositions concerning facts will be promoted to the dignity of science, regardless of their relevance, as long as they result from a correct use of method. Since the ocean of facts is infinite, a prodigious expansion of science in the sociological sense becomes possible, giving employment to scientistic technicians and leading to the fantastic accumulation of irrelevant knowledge through huge "research projects" whose most interesting feature is the quantifiable expense that has gone into their production. The temptation is great to look more closely at these luxury flowers of late positivism and to add a few reflections on the garden of Academus in which they grow; but theoretical asceticism will not allow such horticultural pleasures. The present concern is with the principle that all facts are equal—as on occasion it has been formulated—if they are methodically ascertained. This equality of facts is independent of the method used in the special case. The accumulation of irrelevant facts does not require the application of statistical methods: it may quite as well occur under the pretext of critical methods in political history, description of institutions, history of ideas, or in the various branches of philology. The accumulation of theoretically undigested, and perhaps undigestible, facts, the excrescence for which the Germans have coined the term *Materialhuberei*, thus, is the first of the manifestations of positivism; and, because of its pervasiveness, it is of much greater importance than such attractive oddities as the "unified science."

The accumulation of irrelevant facts, however, is inextricably interwoven with other phenomena. Major research enterprises which contain nothing but irrelevant materials are rare, indeed, if they exist at all. Even the worst instance will contain a page here and there of relevant analysis, and there may be grains of gold buried in them that wait for accidental discovery by a scholar who recognizes their value. For the phenomenon of positivism occurs in a civilization with theoretical traditions; and a case of complete irrelevance is practically impossible because, under environmental pressure, the most bulky and worthless collection of materials must hang on a thread, however thin, that connects it with the tradition. Even the staunchest positivist will find it difficult to write a completely worthless book about American constitutional law as long as with any conscientiousness he follows the lines of reasoning and precedents indicated by the decisions of the Supreme Court; even though the book be a dry reportage, and not relate the reasoning of the judges (who are not always the best of theorists) to a critical theory of politics and law, the material will compel submission at least to its own system of relevance.

Much deeper than by the easily recognizable accumulation of trivialities has science been destroyed by the second manifestation of positivism, that is, by the operation on relevant materials under defective theoretical principles. Highly respectable scholars have invested an immense erudition into the digestion of historical materials, and their effort has gone largely to waste because their principles of selection and interpretation had no proper theoretical foundation but derived from the *Zeitgeist*, political preferences, or personal idiosyn-

crasies. Into this class belong the histories of Greek philosophy which from their sources primarily extracted a "contribution" to the foundation of Western science; the treatises on
Plato which discovered in him a precursor of Neo-Kantian
logic or, according to the political fashions of the time, a constitutionalist, a utopian, a socialist, or a Fascist; the histories
of political ideas which defined politics in terms of Western
constitutionalism and then were unable to discover much political theory in the Middle Ages; or the other variant which
discovered in the Middle Ages a good deal of "contribution"
to constitutional doctrine but completely ignored the block of
political sectarian movements which culminated in the Reformation; or a giant enterprise like Gierke's *Genossenschafts-
recht* that was badly vitiated by its author's conviction that
the history of political and legal thought was providentially
moving toward its climax in his own theory of the *Realperson*.
In cases of this class the damage is not due to an accumulation
of worthless materials; on the contrary, the treatises of this
type quite frequently are still indispensable because of their
reliable informations concerning facts (bibliographical references, critical establishment of texts, etc.). The damage is
rather done through interpretation. The content of a source
may be reported correctly as far as it goes, and nevertheless the
report may create an entirely false picture because essential
parts are omitted. And they are omitted because the uncritical
principles of interpretation do not permit recognizing them as
essential. Uncritical opinion, private or public (*doxa* in the
Platonic sense), cannot substitute for theory in science.

The third manifestation of positivism was the development
of methodology, especially in the half-century from 1870 to
1920. The movement was distinctly a phase of positivism in so
far as the perversion of relevance, through the shift from theory to method, was the very principle by which it lived. At
the same time, however, it was instrumental in overcoming

positivism because it generalized the relevance of method and thereby regained the understanding of the specific adequacy of different methods for different sciences. Thinkers like Husserl or Cassirer, for instance, were still positivists of the Comtean persuasion with regard to their philosophy of history; but Husserl's critique of psychologism and Cassirer's philosophy of symbolic forms were important steps toward the restoration of theoretical relevance. The movement as a whole, therefore, is far too complex to admit of generalizations without careful and extensive qualifications. Only one problem can, and must, be selected because it has a specific bearing on the destruction of science, that is, the attempt at making political science (and the social sciences in general) "objective" through a methodologically rigorous exclusion of all "value-judgments."

In order to arrive at clarity about the issue, it must first of all be realized that the terms "value-judgment" and "value-free" science were not part of the philosophical vocabulary before the second half of the nineteenth century. The notion of a value-judgment (*Werturteil*) is meaningless in itself; it gains its meaning from a situation in which it is opposed to judgments concerning facts (*Tatsachenurteile*). And this situation was created through the positivistic conceit that only propositions concerning facts of the phenomenal world were "objective," while judgments concerning the right order of soul and society were "subjective." Only propositions of the first type could be considered "scientific," while propositions of the second type expressed personal preferences and decisions, incapable of critical verification and therefore devoid of objective validity. This classification made sense only if the positivistic dogma was accepted on principle; and it could be accepted only by thinkers who did not master the classic and Christian science of man. For neither classic nor Christian ethics and politics contain "value-judgments" but elaborate, empirically and critically, the problems of order which derive

from philosophical anthropology as part of a general ontology. Only when ontology as a science was lost, and when consequently ethics and politics could no longer be understood as
sciences of the order in which human nature reaches its maximal actualization, was it possible for this realm of knowledge
to become suspect as a field of subjective, uncritical opinion.

In so far as the methodologists accepted the positivistic
dogma, they participated in the destruction of science. At the
same time, however, they tried valiantly to save the historical
and social sciences from the disrepute into which they were
liable to fall because of the destruction in which they participated. When the *episteme* is ruined, men do not stop talking
about politics; but they now must express themselves in the
mode of *doxa*. The so-called value-judgments could become a
serious concern for methodologists because, in philosophical
language, they were *doxai*, uncritical opinions concerning the
problem of order; and the methodologists' attempt to make
the social sciences again respectable by eliminating current
uncritical opining did at least awaken the consciousness of
critical standards, even though it could not re-establish a science of order. Hence, the theory of "value-judgments" as well
as the attempt to establish a "value-free" science were ambivalent in their effects. In so far as the attack on value-judgments was an attack on uncritical opinion under the guise of
political science, it had the wholesome effect of theoretical
purification. In so far as under the concept of value-judgments
was subsumed the whole body of classic and Christian metaphysics, and especially of philosophical anthropology, the
attack could result in nothing less than a confession that a
science of human and social order did not exist.

The variety of concrete attempts has to a large part lost its
interest now that the great methodological battles have sub-
sided. They were generically governed by the principle of

pushing the "values" out of science into the position of unquestioned axioms or hypotheses. Under the assumption, for instance, that the "state" was a value, political history and political science would be legitimated as "objective" in so far as they explored motivations, actions, and conditions that had a bearing on creation, preservation, and extinction of states. Obviously, the principle would lead to dubious results if the legitimating value was put at the discretion of the scientist. If science was defined as exploration of facts in relation to a value, there would be as many political histories and political sciences as there were scholars with different ideas about what was valuable. The facts that are treated as relevant because they have a bearing on the values of a progressivist will not be the same facts that are considered relevant by a conservative; and the relevant facts of a liberal economist will not be the relevant facts of a Marxist. Neither the most scrupulous care in keeping the concrete work "value-free" nor the most conscientious observation of critical method in establishing facts and causal relations could prevent the sinking of historical and political sciences into a morass of relativism. As a matter of fact, the idea was advanced, and could find wide consent, that every generation would have to write history anew because the "values" which determined the selection of problems and materials had changed. If the resulting mess was not worse than it actually was, the reason must again be sought in the pressure of a civilizational tradition which held the diversification of uncritical opinion within its general frame.

3

The movement of methodology, as far as political science is concerned, ran to the end of its immanent logic in the person and work of Max Weber. A full characterization cannot be attempted in the present context. Only a few of the lines that mark him as a thinker between the end and a new beginning will be traced.

A value-free science meant to Weber the exploration of causes and effects, the construction of ideal types that would permit distinguishing regularities of institutions as well as deviations from them, and especially the construction of typical causal relations. Such a science would not be in a position to tell anybody whether he should be an economic liberal or a socialist, a democratic constitutionalist or a Marxist revolutionary, but it could tell him what the consequences would be if he tried to translate the values of his preference into political practice. On the one side, there were the "values" of political order beyond critical evaluation; on the other side, there was a science of the structure of social reality that might be used as technical knowledge by a politician. In sharpening the issue of a "value-free" science to this pragmatic point, Weber moved the debate beyond methodological squabbles again to the order of relevance. He wanted science because he wanted clarity about the world in which he passionately participated; he was headed again on the road toward essence. The search for truth, however, was cut short at the level of pragmatic action. In the intellectual climate of the methodological debate the "values" had to be accepted as unquestionable, and the search could not advance to the contemplation of order. The *ratio* of science extended, for Weber, not to the principles but only to the causality of action.

The new sense of theoretical relevance could express itself, therefore, only in the creation of the categories of "responsibility" and "demonism" in politics. Weber recognized the "values" for what they were, that is, as ordering ideas for political action, but he accorded them the status of "demonic" decisions beyond rational argument. Science could grapple with the demonism of politics only by making politicians aware of the consequences of their actions and awakening in them the sense of responsibility. This Weberian "ethics of responsibility" is not at all negligible. It was calculated to put a damper on the revolutionary ardor of opinionated political intellectuals, especially after 1918; to bring it home that ideals justify neither the means nor the results of action, that action involves in guilt, and that the responsibility for political effects rests squarely on the man who makes himself a cause. Moreover, by the diagnosis as "demonic" it revealed that unquestionable "values" cannot be traced to rational sources of order and that the politics of the age had indeed become a field of demonic disorder. The accomplished smoothness by which this aspect of Weber's work was, and is, ignored by those whom it might concern is perhaps the best proof of its importance.

If Weber had done nothing but revealed that a "value-free" political science is not a science of order and that "values" are demonic decisions, the grandeur of his work (that is more sensed than understood) might be open to doubt. The ascent toward essence would have stopped at the point at which the side road branches off which conventionally is marked as "existentialism"—an escape for the bewildered that in recent years has become internationally fashionable through the work of Sartre. Weber, however, went much further—though the interpreter finds himself in the difficult position that he must extract the achievement from the intellectual conflicts and contradictions in which Weber involved himself. The approach to the problem of a value-free science that was just described compels more than one question. Weber's conception of science, for instance, assumed a social relation between scientist and politician, activated in the institution of a university, where the scientist as teacher will inform his students, the prospective *homines politici*, about the structure of political reality. The question may be asked: What purpose should such information have? The science of Weber supposedly left the political values of the students untouched, since the values were beyond science. The political principles of the students could not be formed by a science which did not extend to principles of order. Could it perhaps have the indirect effect of inviting the students to revise their values when they realized what unsuspected, and perhaps undesired, consequences their political ideas would have in practice? But in that case the values of the students would not be quite so demonically fixed. An appeal to judgment would be possible, and what could a judgment that resulted in reasoned preference of value over value be but a value-judgment? Were reasoned value-judgments possible after all? The teaching of a value-free science of politics in a university would be a senseless enterprise unless it were calculated to influence the values of the students by putting at their disposition an objective knowledge of political reality. In so far as Weber was a great teacher, he gave the lie to his idea of values as demonic decisions.

To what extent his method of teaching could be effective is another matter. In the first place, it was a teaching by indirection because he shunned an explicit statement of positive principles of order; and, in the second place, the teaching even through direct elaboration of principles could not be effective if the student was indeed demonically fixed in his attitudes. Weber, as an educator, could rely only on shame (the Aristotelian *aidos*) in the student as the sentiment that would induce rational consideration. But what if the student was beyond shame? If the appeal to his sense of responsibility would only make him uncomfortable without producing a change of attitude? Or if it would not even make him uncomfortable but rather fall back on what Weber called an "ethics of intention" (*Gesinnungsethik*), that is, on the thesis that his creed contained its own justification, that the consequences did not matter if the intention of action was right? This question, again, was not clarified by Weber. As the model case for his "ethics of intention" he used a not-too-well-defined Christian "other-worldly" morality; he never touched the problem whether the demonic values were not perhaps demonic precisely because they partook of his "ethics of intention" rather than of his "ethics of responsibility," because they had arrogated the quality of a divine command to a human velleity. A discussion of such questions would have been possible only on the level of a philosophical anthropology from which Weber shied away. Nevertheless, while he shied away from a discussion, he had made his decision for entering into rational conflict with values through the mere fact of his enterprise.

The rational conflict with the unquestionable values of political intellectuals was inherent in his enterprise of an objective science of politics. The original conception of a value-free science was dissolving. To the methodologists preceding Max Weber, a historical or social science could be value-free because its object was constituted by "reference to a value" (*wertbeziehende Methode*); within the field thus constituted the scientist was then supposed to work without value-judgments. Weber recognized that there was a plurality of conflicting "values" current in the politics of his time; each of them might be used to constitute an "object." The result would be the aforementioned relativism, and political science would be degraded to an apology for the dubious fancies of political intellectuals, as at the time it was and as to a very considerable extent it still is. How did he escape such degradation—for escape he certainly did? If none of the conflicting values constituted for him the field of science, if he preserved his critical integrity against the current political values, what then were the values which constituted his science? An exhaustive answer to these questions lies beyond the present purpose. Only the principle of his technique will be illustrated. The "objectivity" of Weber's science, such as there was, could be derived only from the authentic principles of order as they had been discovered and elaborated in the history of mankind. Since in the intellectual situation of Weber the existence of a science of order could not be admitted, its content (or as much of it as was possible) had to be introduced by recognizing its historical expressions as facts and causal factors in history. While Weber as a methodologist of value-free science would profess to have no argument against a political intellectual who had "demonically" settled on Marxism as the "value" of his preference, he could blandly engage in a study of Protestant ethics and show that certain religious convictions rather than the class struggle played an important role in the formation of capitalism. In the preceding pages it has been repeatedly stressed that the arbitrariness of method did not degenerate into complete irrelevance of scientific production, because the pressure of theoretical traditions remained a determining factor in the selection of materials and problems. This pressure, one might say, was erected by Weber into a principle. The three volumes, for instance, of his sociology of religion threw a massive bulk of more or less clearly seen verities about human and social order into the debate about the structure of reality. By pointing to the undisputable fact that verities about order were factors in the order of reality—and not perhaps only lust for power and wealth or fear and fraud—a tentative objectivity of science could be regained, even though the principles had to be introduced by the back door of "beliefs" in competition, and in rationally insoluble conflict, with Weber's contemporary "values."

Again, Weber ignored the theoretical difficulties into which this procedure involved him. If the "objective" study of historical processes showed that, for instance, the materialistic interpretation of history was wrong, then obviously there existed a standard of objectivity in science which precluded the constitution of the object of science by "referring" facts and problems to the "value" of a Marxist; or—without methodological jargon—a scholar could not be a Marxist. But, if critical objectivity made it impossible for a scholar to be a Marxist, could then any man be a Marxist without surrendering the standards of critical objectivity that he would be obliged to observe as a responsible human being? There are no answers to such questions in Weber's work. The time had not yet come to state flatly that "historical materialism" is not a theory but a falsification of history or that a "materialistic" interpreter of politics is an ignoramus who had better bone up on elementary facts. As a second component in the "demonism" of values there begins to emerge, not acknowledged as such by Weber, a goodly portion of ignorance. And the political intellectual who "demonically" decides himself for his "value" begins suspiciously to look like a megalomaniac ignoramus. It would seem that "demonism" is a quality which a man possesses in inverse proportion to the radius of his relevant knowledge.

The whole complex of ideas—of "values," "reference to values," "value-judgments," and "value-free science"— seemed on the point of disintegration. An "objectivity" of science had been regained that plainly did not fit into the pattern of the methodological debate. And, yet, even the studies on sociology of religion could not induce Weber to take the decisive step toward a science of order. The ultimate reason of his hesitation, if not fear, is perhaps impenetrable; but the technical point at which he stopped can be clearly discerned. His studies on sociology of religion have always aroused admiration as a tour de force, if not for other reasons. The amount of materials which he mastered in these voluminous studies on Protestantism, Confucianism, Taoism, Hinduism, Buddhism, Jainism, Israel, and Judaism, to be completed by a study on Islam, is indeed awe-inspiring. In the face of such impressive performance it has perhaps not been sufficiently observed that the series of these studies receives its general tone through a significant omission, that is, of pre-Reformation Christianity. The reason of the omission seems to be obvious. One can hardly engage in a serious study of medieval Christianity without discovering among its "values" the belief in a rational science of human and social order and especially of natural law. Moreover, this science was not simply a belief, but it was actually elaborated as a work of reason. Here Weber would have run into the fact of a science of order, just as he would if he had seriously occupied himself with Greek philosophy. Weber's readiness to introduce verities about order as historical facts stopped short of Greek and medieval metaphysics. In order to degrade the politics of Plato, Aristotle, or St. Thomas to the rank of "values" among others, a conscientious scholar would first have to show that their claim to be science was unfounded. And that attempt is self-defeating. By the time the would-be critic has penetrated the meaning of metaphysics with sufficient thoroughness to make his criticism weighty, he will have become a metaphysician himself. The attack on metaphysics can be undertaken with a good conscience only from the safe distance of imperfect knowledge. The horizon of Weber's social science was immense; all the more does his caution in coming too close to its decisive center reveal his positivistic limitations.

Hence, the result of Weber's work was ambiguous. He had reduced the principle of a value-free science *ad absurdum*. The idea of a value-free science whose object would be constituted by "reference to a value" could be realized only under the condition that a scientist was willing to decide on a "value" for reference. If the scientist refused to decide on a "value," if he treated all "values" as equal (as Max Weber did), if, moreover, he treated them as social facts among others—then there were no "values" left which could constitute the object of science, because they had become part of the object itself. This abolition of the "values" as the constituents of science led to a theoretically impossible situation because the object of science has a "constitution" after all, that is, the essence toward which we are moving in our search for truth. Since the positivistic hangover, however, did not permit the admission of a science of essence, of a true *episteme*, the principles of order had to be introduced as historical facts. When Weber built the great edifice of his "sociology" (i.e., the positivistic escape from the science of order), he did not seriously consider all "values" as equal. He did not indulge in a worthless trash collection but displayed quite sensible preferences for phenomena that were "important" in the history of mankind; he could distinguish quite well between major civilizations and less important side developments and equally well between "world religions" and unimportant religious phenomena. In the absence of a reasoned principle of theoretization he let himself be guided not by "values" but by the *auctoritas majorum* and his own sensitiveness for excellence.

Thus far the work of Weber can be characterized as a successful attempt to disengage political science from the irrelevances of methodology and to restore it to theoretical order. The new theory toward which he was moving, however, could not become explicit because he religiously observed the positivistic taboo on metaphysics. Instead, something else became explicit; for Weber wanted to be explicit on his principles as a theorist should be. Throughout his work he struggled with an explication of his theory under the title of construction of "types." The various phases through which this struggle passed cannot be considered on this occasion. In the last phase he used types of "rational action" as the standard types and constructed the other types as deviations from rationality. The procedure suggested itself because Weber understood history as an evolution toward rationality and his own age as the hitherto highest point of "rational self-determination" of man. In various degrees of completeness he carried this idea out for economic, political, and religious history, most completely for the history of music. The general conception obviously derived from Comte's philosophy of history; and Weber's own interpretation of history might justly be understood as the last of the great positivistic systems. In Weber's execution of the plan, however, there can be sensed a new tone. The evolution of mankind toward the rationality of positive science was for Comte a distinctly progressive development; for Weber it was a process of disenchantment (*Entzauberung*) and de-divinization (*Entgöttlichung*) of the world. By the overtones of his regret that divine enchantment had seeped out of the world, by his resignation to rationalism as a fate to be borne but not desired, by the occasional complaint that his soul was not attuned to the divine (*religiös unmusikalisch*), he rather betrayed his brotherhood in the sufferings of Nietzsche—though, in spite of his confession, his soul was sufficiently attuned to the divine not to follow Nietzsche into his tragic revolt. He knew what he wanted but somehow could not break through to it. He saw the promised land but was not permitted to enter it.

4

In the work of Max Weber positivism had come to its end, and the lines on which the restoration of political science would have to move became visible. The correlation between a constituent "value" and a constituted "value-free" science had broken down; the "value-judgments" were back in science in the form of the "legitimating beliefs" which created units of social order. The last stronghold was Weber's conviction that history moved toward a type of rationalism which relegated religion and metaphysics into the realm of the "irrational." And that was not much of a stronghold as soon as it was understood that nobody was obliged to enter it; that one simply could turn around and rediscover the rationality of metaphysics in general and of philosophical anthropology in particular, that is, the areas of science from which Max Weber had kept studiously aloof.

The formula for the remedy is simpler than its application. Science is not the singlehanded achievement of this or that individual scholar; it is a co-operative effort. Effective work is possible only within a tradition of intellectual culture. When science is as thoroughly ruined as it was around 1900, the mere recovery of theoretical craftsmanship is a considerable task, to say nothing of the amounts of materials that must be reworked in order to reconstruct the order of relevance in facts and problems. Moreover, the personal difficulties must not be overlooked; the exposition of apparently wild, new ideas will inevitably meet with resistance in the environment. An example will help to understand the nature of these various difficulties.

Weber, as has just been set forth, still conceived history as an increase of rationalism in the positivistic sense. From the position of a science of order, however, the exclusion of the *scientia prima* from the realm of reason is not an increase but a decrease of rationalism. What Weber, in the wake of Comte, understood as modern rationalism would have to be reinterpreted as modern irrationalism. This inversion of the socially accepted meaning of terms would arouse a certain hostility. But a reinterpretation could not stop at this point. The rejection of sciences that were already developed and the return to a lower level of rationality obviously must have experientially deep-seated motivations. A closer inquiry would reveal certain religious experiences at the bottom of the unwillingness to recognize the *ratio* of ontology and philosophical anthropology; and, as a matter of fact, in the 1890's began the exploration of socialism as a religious movement, an exploration which later developed into the extensive study of totalitarian movements as a new "myth" or religion. The inquiry would, furthermore, lead to the general problem of a connection between types of rationality and types of religious experience. Some religious experiences would have to be classified as higher, others as lower, by the objective criterion of the degree of rationality which they admit in the interpretation of reality. The religious experiences of the Greek mystic philosophers and of Christianity would rank high because they allow the unfolding of metaphysics; the religious experiences of Comte and Marx would rank low because they prohibit the asking of metaphysical questions. Such considerations would radically upset the positivistic conception of an evolution from an early religious or theological phase of mankind to rationalism and science. Not only would the evolution go from a higher to a lower degree of rationalism, at least for the modern period, but, in addition, this decline of reason would have to be understood as the consequence of religious retrogression. An interpretation of Western history that had grown over centuries would have to be revolutionized; and a revolution of this magnitude would meet the opposition of "progressives" who all of a sudden would find themselves in the position of retrogressive irrationalists.

The possibilities of a reinterpretation of rationalism, as well as of the positivistic conception of history, were put in the subjunctive in order to indicate the hypothetical character of a restoration of political science at the turn of the century. Ideas of the suggested type were afloat; but from the certainty that something was badly wrong in the state of science to a precise understanding of the nature of the evil there was a long way; and equally long was the way from intelligent surmises about the direction in which one had to move to the attainment of the goal. A good number of conditions had to be fulfilled before the propositions in this case could be translated into the indicative mood. The understanding of ontology as well as the craftsmanship of metaphysical speculation had to be regained, and especially philosophical anthropology as a science had to be re-established. By the standards thus regained it was possible to define with precision the technical points of irrationality in the positivistic position. For this purpose the works of the leading positivistic thinkers had to be analyzed with care in order to find their critical rejections of rational argument; one had, for instance, to show the passages in the works of Comte and Marx where these thinkers recognized the validity of metaphysical questions but refused to consider them because such consideration would make their irrational opining impossible. When the study proceeded further to the motivations of irrationalism, positivistic thinking had to be determined as a variant of theologizing, again on the basis of the sources; and the underlying religious experiences had to be diagnosed. This diagnosis could be conducted successfully only if a general theory of religious phenomena was sufficiently elaborated to allow the subsumption of the concrete case under a type. The further generalization concerning the connection of degrees of rationality with religious experiences, and the comparison with Greek and Christian instances, required a renewed study of Greek philosophy that would bring out the connection between the unfolding of Greek metaphysics and the religious experiences of the philosophers who developed it; and a further study of medieval metaphysics had to establish the corresponding connection for the Christian case. It had, moreover, to demonstrate the characteristic differences between Greek and Christian metaphysics which could be attributed to the religious differences. And when all these preparatory studies were made, when critical concepts for treatment of the problems were formed, and the propositions were supported by the sources, the final task had to be faced of searching for a theoretically intelligible order of history into which these variegated phenomena could be organized.

This task of restoration has, indeed, been undertaken; and today it has reached the point where one can say that at least the foundations for a new science of order have been laid. A detailed description of the far-flung enterprise lies beyond the present purpose—and besides it would have to grow into a compendious history of science in the first half of the twentieth century.[1] The following lectures on the problem of representation intend to introduce the reader to this movement as well as to the promise which it holds for a restoration of political science.

1. The intellectual history of the first half of the twentieth century is extremely complex because it is the history of a slow recovery (with many trials that have ended in impasses) from the thorough destruction of intellectual culture in the late nineteenth century. A critical study of this process would be perhaps premature as long as the dust of the struggle is still flying; and, in fact, no such comprehensive study has hitherto been attempted. There exists, however, a recent introduction to contemporary philosophy which (in spite of certain technical shortcomings) demonstrates how much can be done even today; it is I. M. Bochenski's *Europäische Philosophie der Gegenwart* (Bern, 1947). In his interpretation the author is guided by the two mottoes on the title-page of his book—Marcus Aurelius' "The philosopher, this priest and helper of the Gods" and Bergson's "Philosophy, too, has its scribes and pharisees." The various philosophies are ranked according to their value as ontologies, from the lowest to the highest, under the chapter headings of "Matter," "Idea," "Life," "Essence," "Existence," "Being." The last chapter, on the philosophies of being, deals with the English and German metaphysicians (Samuel Alexander, Alfred N. Whitehead, Nicolai Hartmann) and the Neo-Thomists. The first chapter deals with the lowest-ranking philosophies, from the bottom up with Bertrand Russell, neo-positivism, and dialectical materialism.

I

REPRESENTATION AND EXISTENCE

✣

1

POLITICAL science is suffering from a difficulty that originates in its very nature as a science of man in historical existence. For man does not wait for science to have his life explained to him, and when the theorist approaches social reality he finds the field pre-empted by what may be called the self-interpretation of society. Human society is not merely a fact, or an event, in the external world to be studied by an observer like a natural phenomenon. Though it has externality as one of its important components, it is as a whole a little world, a cosmion, illuminated with meaning from within by the human beings who continuously create and bear it as the mode and condition of their self-realization. It is illuminated through an elaborate symbolism, in various degrees of compactness and differentiation—from rite, through myth, to theory—and this symbolism illuminates it with meaning in so far as the symbols make the internal structure of such a cosmion, the relations between its members and groups of members, as well as its existence as a whole, transparent for the mystery of human existence. The self-illumination of society through symbols is an integral part of social reality, and one may even say its essential part, for through such symbolization the members of a society experience it as more than an accident or a convenience; they experience it as of their human essence. And, inversely, the symbols express the experience that man is fully man by virtue of his participation in a whole which transcends his particular existence, by virtue of his par-

27

ticipation in the *xynon*, the common, as Heraclitus called it, the first Western thinker who differentiated this concept. As a consequence, every human society has an understanding of itself through a variety of symbols, sometimes highly differentiated language symbols, independent of political science; and such self-understanding precedes historically by millenniums the emergence of political science, of the *episteme politike* in the Aristotelian sense. Hence, when political science begins, it does not begin with a *tabula rasa* on which it can inscribe its concepts; it will inevitably start from the rich body of self-interpretation of a society and proceed by critical clarification of socially pre-existent symbols. When Aristotle wrote his *Ethics* and *Politics*, when he constructed his concepts of the polis, of the constitution, the citizen, the various forms of government, of justice, of happiness, etc., he did not invent these terms and endow them with arbitrary meanings; he took rather the symbols which he found in his social environment, surveyed with care the variety of meanings which they had in common parlance, and ordered and clarified these meanings by the criteria of his theory.[1]

These preliminaries do by no means exhaust the peculiar situation of political science, but they have gone far enough for the more immediate purpose. They will allow a few theoretical conclusions which, in their turn, can be applied to the topic of representation.

When a theorist reflects on his own theoretical situation, he finds himself faced with two sets of symbols: the language symbols that are produced as an integral part of the social cosmion in the process of its self-illumination and the language symbols of political science. Both are related with each other in so far as the second set is developed out of the first one through the process that provisionally was called critical clarification. In the course of this process some of the symbols

1. Aristotle *Politics* 1280a7 ff.

that occur in reality will be dropped because they cannot be put to any use in the economy of science, while new symbols will be developed in theory for the critically adequate description of symbols that are part of reality. If the theorist, for instance, describes the Marxian idea of the realm of freedom, to be established by a Communist revolution, as an immanentist hypostasis of a Christian eschatological symbol, the symbol "realm of freedom" is part of reality; it is part of a secular movement of which the Marxist movement is a subdivision, while such terms as "immanentist," "hypostasis," and "eschatology" are concepts of political science. The terms used in the description do not occur in the reality of the Marxist movement, while the symbol "realm of freedom" is useless in critical science. Hence, neither are there two sets of terms with different meanings nor is there one set of terms with two distinct sets of meanings; there exist rather two sets of symbols with a large area of overlapping phonemes. Moreover, the symbols in reality are themselves to a considerable extent the result of clarifying processes so that the two sets will also approach each other frequently with regard to their meanings and sometimes even achieve identity. This complicated situation inevitably is a source of confusion; in particular, it is the source of the illusion that the symbols used in political reality are theoretical concepts.

This confusing illusion unfortunately has rather deeply corroded contemporary political science. One does not hesitate, for instance, to speak of a "contract theory of government," or of a "theory of sovereignty," or of a "Marxist theory of history," while in fact it is rather doubtful whether any of these so-called theories can qualify as theory in the critical sense; and voluminous histories of "political theory" bring an exposition of symbols which, for the larger part, have very little theoretical about them. Such confusion even destroys some of the gains that already were made in political science in antiquity. Take, for instance, the so-called contract theory. In this case the fact is ignored that Plato has given a very thorough analysis of the contract symbol. He not only established its nontheoretical character but also explored the type of experience that lies at its root. Moreover, he introduced the technical term *doxa* for the class of symbols of which the "contract theory" is an instance in order to distinguish them from the symbols of theory.[2] Today theorists do not use the term *doxa* for this purpose, nor have they developed an equivalent—the distinction is lost. Instead the term "ideology" has come into vogue which in some respects is related to the Platonic *doxa*. But precisely this term has become a further source of confusion because under the pressure of what Mannheim has called the *allgemeine Ideologieverdacht*, the general suspicion of ideology, its meaning has been extended so far as to cover all types of symbols used in propositions on politics, including the symbols of theory themselves; there are numerous political scientists today who would even call the Platonic-Aristotelian *episteme* an ideology.

A further symptom of such confusion is certain discussion habits. More than once in a discussion of a political topic it has happened that a student—and for that matter not always a student—would ask me how I defined fascism, or socialism, or some other ism of that order. And more than once I had to surprise the questioner—who apparently as part of a college education had picked up the idea that science was a warehouse of dictionary definitions—by my assurance that I did not feel obliged to indulge in such definitions, because movements of the suggested type, together with their symbolisms, were part of reality, that only concepts could be defined but not reality, and that it was highly doubtful whether the language symbols in question could be critically clarified to such a point that they were of any cognitive use in science.

The ground is now prepared for approaching the topic of

2. Plato *Republic* 358e–367e.

representation proper. The foregoing reflections will have made it clear that the task will not be quite simple if the inquiry is conducted in accordance with critical standards of a search for truth. Theoretical concepts and the symbols that are part of reality must be carefully distinguished; in the transition from reality to theory the criteria employed in the process of clarification must be well defined; and the cognitive value of the resulting concepts must be tested by placing them in larger theoretical contexts. The method thus outlined is substantially the Aristotelian procedure.

2

It will be appropriate to begin with the elemental aspects of the topic. In order to determine what is theoretically elemental, it will be well to recall the beginning of this lecture. A political society was characterized as a cosmion illuminated from within; this characterization, however, was qualified by stressing externality as one of its important components. The cosmion has its inner realm of meaning; but this realm exists tangibly in the external world in human beings who have bodies and through their bodies participate in the organic and inorganic externality of the world. A political society can dissolve not only through the disintegration of the beliefs that make it an acting unit in history; it can also be destroyed through the dispersion of its members in such a manner that communication between them becomes physically impossible or, most radically, through their physical extermination; it also can suffer serious damage, partial destruction of tradition, and prolonged paralysis through extermination or suppression of the active members who constitute the political and intellectual ruling minorities of a society. External existence of society in this sense is intended when, for reasons that will appear presently, we speak of the theoretically elemental aspect of our topic.

In political debate, in the press, and in the publicist literature, countries like the United States, the United Kingdom, France, Switzerland, the Low Countries, or the Scandinavian kingdoms are habitually referred to as countries with representative institutions. In such contexts the term occurs as a symbol in political reality. When a man who uses the symbol would be requested to explain what he means by it, he would almost certainly respond by saying that the institutions of a country will qualify as representative when the members of the legislative assembly hold their membership by virtue of popular election. When the questioning is extended to the executive, he will accept the American election of a chief executive by the people, but he will also agree to the English system of a committee of the parliamentary majority as the ministry, or to the Swiss system of having the executive elected by the two houses in common session; and probably he will not find the representative character impaired by a monarch, as long as the monarch can act only with the countersignature of a responsible minister. When he is urged to be a bit more explicit about what he means by popular election, he will primarily consider the election of a representative by all persons of age who are resident in a territorial district; but he will probably not deny the representative character when women are excluded from suffrage or when, under a system of proportional representation, the constituencies are personal instead of territorial. He, finally, may suggest that elections should be reasonably frequent, and he will mention parties as the organizers and mediators of the election procedure.

What can the theorist do with an answer of this type in science? Does it have any cognitive value?

Obviously, the answer is not negligible. To be sure, the existence of the enumerated countries must be taken for granted without too many questions about what makes them exist or what existence means. Nevertheless, light falls on an area of institutions within an existential framework, even though that framework itself remains in the shadow. There exist, indeed, several countries whose institutions can be subsumed under the adumbrated type; and, if the exploration of institutions is relevant at all, this answer certainly suggests a formidable body of scientific knowledge. Moreover, this body of knowledge exists as a massive fact of science in the form of numerous monographic studies on the institutions of single countries, describing the ramifications and auxiliary institutions which are necessary for the operation of a modern representative government, as well as in the form of comparative studies which elaborate the type and its variants. There can, furthermore, be no doubt about the theoretical relevance of such studies, at least on principle, because the external existence of a political society is part of its ontological structure. Whatever their relevance may prove to be when they are placed in a larger theoretical context, the types of external realization of a society will have at least some relevance.

In the theoretization of representative institutions on this level, the concepts which enter into the construction of the descriptive type refer to simple data of the external world. They refer to geographical districts, to human beings who are resident in them, to men and women, to their age, to their voting which consists in placing check marks on pieces of paper by the side of names printed on them, to operations of counting and calculation that will result in the designation of other human beings as representatives, to the behavior of representatives that will result in formal acts recognizable as such through external data, etc. Because the concepts on this level are unproblematic in terms of the internal self-interpretation of a society, this aspect of our topic may be considered elemental; and the descriptive type of representation that can be developed on this level, therefore, shall be called the **elemental type.**

The relevance of the elemental approach to the topic is established on principle. The actual extent of its cognitive value, however, can be measured only by placing the type into the previously suggested larger theoretical context. The elemental type, as we said, casts light only on an area of institutions within an existential framework, to be taken for granted without questions. Hence, a few questions must now be raised with regard to the area that hitherto remained in shadow.

3

In raising these questions, again the Aristotelian procedure of examining symbols as they occur in reality will be followed. A suitable subject for such questioning is the representative character of the Soviet institutions. The Soviet Union has a constitution, even beautifully written, providing for institutions which, on the whole, can be subsumed under the elemental type. Nevertheless, opinion concerning its representative character is sharply divided between Western democrats and Communists. Westerners will say that the mechanism of representation alone will not do, that the voter must have a genuine choice, and that the party monopoly provided by the Soviet constitution makes a choice impossible. Communists will say that the true representative must have the interest of the people at heart, that the exclusion of parties representing special interests is necessary in order to make the institutions truly representative, and that only countries where the monopoly of representation is secured for the Communist party are genuine people's democracies. The argument, thus, hinges on the mediatory function of the party in the process of representation.

The issue is too unclear for rendering immediate judgment. The situation rather invites a little deeper stirring, and, indeed, one can easily add to the confusion by recalling that at the time of the foundation of the American Republic eminent statesmen were of the opinion that true representation was

possible only when there were no parties at all. Other thinkers, furthermore, will attribute the functioning of the English
two-party system to the fact that originally the two parties
were, indeed, two factions of the English aristocracy; and
still others will find in the American two-party system an ulterior homogeneousness that lets the two parties appear as
factions of one party. In summarizing the variety of opinion,
hence, one can form the series: a representative system is truly
representative when there are no parties, when there is one
party, when there are two or more parties, when the two parties can be considered factions of one party. In order to complete the picture, there may be, finally, added the type concept
of the pluralistic party state that came into vogue after the
first World War with its implication that a representative
system will not work if there are two or more parties who
disagree on points of principle.

From this variety of opinions it will be possible to draw the
following conclusions. The elemental type of representative
institutions does not exhaust the problem of representation.
Through the conflict of opinions there can be discerned the
consensus that the procedure of representation is meaningful
only when certain requirements concerning its substance are
fulfilled and that the establishment of the procedure does not
automatically provide the desired substance. There is, furthermore, a consensus that certain mediatory institutions, the parties, have something to do with securing or corrupting this
substance. Beyond this point, however, the issue becomes con-
fused. The substance in question is vaguely associated with
the will of the people, but what precisely is meant by the symbol "people" does not become clear. This symbol must be
stored away for later examination. Moreover, the disagreement on the number of parties that will, or will not, guarantee
the flow of the substance suggests an insufficiently analyzed
ulterior issue that will not come into grasp by counting par-

ties. Hence, a type concept like the "one-party state" must be considered as theoretically of dubious value; it may have some practical use for brief reference in current political debate, but it is obviously not sufficiently clarified to be of relevance in science. It belongs to the elemental class like the elemental type concept of representative institutions.

These first methodical questions have not led into an impasse, but the gain is inconclusive because too much was netted at a time. The issue must be narrowed down for clarification; and for this purpose further reflection on the tempting subject of the Soviet Union is indicated.

4

While there may be radical disagreement on the question whether the Soviet government represents the people, there can be no doubt whatsoever that the Soviet government represents the Soviet society as a political society in form for action in history. The legislative and administrative acts of the Soviet government are domestically effective in the sense that the governmental commands find obedience with the people, making allowance for the politically irrelevant margin of failure; and the Soviet Union is a power on the historical scene because the Soviet government can effectively operate an enormous military machine fed by the human and material resources of the Soviet society.

At first glance it appears that with such propositions the argument has advanced to theoretically much more fertile ground. For, under the title of political societies in form for action, the clearly distinguishable power units in history come into view. Political societies, in order to be in form for action, must have an internal structure that will enable some of its members—the ruler, the government, the prince, the sovereign, the magistrate, etc., according to the varying terminology of the ages—to find habitual obedience for their acts of command; and these acts must serve the existential necessities of a society, such as the defense of the realm and administration of justice—if a medieval classification of purposes will be allowed. Such societies with their internal organization for action, however, do not exist as cosmic fixtures from eternity but grow in history; this process in which human beings form themselves into a society for action shall be called the articulation of a society. As the result of political articulation we find human beings, the rulers, who can act for the society, men whose acts are not imputed to their own persons but to the society as a whole—with the consequence that, for instance, the pronunciation of a general rule regulating an area of human life will not be understood as an exercise in moral philosophy but will be experienced by the members of the society as the declaration of a rule with obligatory force for themselves. When his acts are effectively imputed in this manner, a person is the representative of a society.

If the meaning of representation in this context shall be based on effective imputation, it will be necessary, however, to distinguish representation from other types of imputation; it will be necessary to clarify the difference between an agent and a representative. By an agent, therefore, shall be understood a person who is empowered by his principal to transact a specific business under instructions, while by a representative shall be understood a person who has power to act for a society by virtue of his position in the structure of the community, without specific instructions for a specified business, and whose acts will not be effectively repudiated by the members of the society. A delegate to the United Nations, for instance, is an agent of his government acting under instructions, while the government that has delegated him is the representative of the respective political society.

5

Obviously, the representative ruler of an articulated society cannot represent it as a whole without standing in some sort of relationship to the other members of the society. Here is a source of difficulties for political science in our time because, under pressure of the democratic symbolism, the resistance to distinguishing between the two relations terminologically has become so strong that it has also affected political theory. Ruling power is ruling power even in a democracy, but one is shy of facing the fact. The government represents the people, and the symbol "people" has absorbed the two meanings which, in medieval language, for instance, could be distinguished without emotional resistance as the "realm" and the "subjects."

This pressure of the democratic symbolism, now, is the last phase of a series of terminological complications that commence in the high Middle Ages with the very beginnings of the articulation of Western political societies. The Magna Carta, for instance, refers to Parliament as the *commune consilium regni nostri*, as "the common council of our realm."[3] Let us examine this formula. It designates Parliament as the council of the realm, not perhaps as a representation of the people, while the realm itself is possessively the king's. The formula is characteristic for an epoch where two periods of social articulation meet. In a first phase the king alone is the representative of the realm, and the sense of this monopoly of representation is preserved in the possessive pronoun attached to the symbol "realm." In a second phase, communes within the realm, the shires, boroughs, and cities, begin to articulate themselves to the point where they are capable of representing themselves for action; and the barons themselves cease to be individual feudatories and also form themselves into the

3. Magna Carta, chap. 12.

baronagium, a commune capable of action as it appears in the *forma securitatis* of the Magna Carta. The details of this complicated process need not be traced; the point of theoretical interest is that the representatives of the articulate communes when they meet in council form communes of a higher order, ultimately the Parliament of two houses, which understands itself as the representative council of a still larger society, of the realm as a whole. With advancing articulation of society, thus, develops a peculiar composite representative, along with a symbolism expressing its internal hierarchical structure.

The weight of representation remained with the king in the centuries following the Magna Carta. The writs of summons of the thirteenth and fourteenth centuries reveal a consistent terminology, recognizing the articulation of society but still drawing the new participants of representation into the royal representation itself. Not only is the realm the king's but the prelates, the magnates, and the cities are also his. Individual merchants, on the other hand, are not included in the representative symbolism; they are not the king's but always "of the realm" or "of the city," that is, of the whole or of an articulate subdivision.[4] Ordinary individual members of the society are plainly "inhabitants" or "fellow-citizens of the realm."[5] The symbol "people" does not appear as signifying a rank in articulation and representation; it is only used, on occasion, as a synonym for realm in a phrase like the "common welfare of the realm."[6]

The melting of this representative hierarchy into one single representative, the king in Parliament, took a considerable time; that such a melting process was under way became theoretically tangible only centuries later, in a famous passage in

4. *Writ of Summons to a 'Colloquium' of Merchants* (1303), in Stubbs, *Select Charters* (8th ed.), p. 500.

5. *Summons of the Archbishop and Clergy to Parliament* (1295) in Stubbs, *op. cit.*, p. 485.

6. *Summons to the Parliament of Lincoln* (1301), in Stubbs, *op. cit.*, p. 499.

the address of Henry VIII to Parliament in Ferrers' case. On that occasion, in 1543, the king said: "We be informed by our Judges that we at no time stand so highly in our estate royal as in the time of Parliament, wherein we as head and you as members are conjoined and knit together into one body politic, so as whatsoever offence or injury (during that time) is offered to the meanest member of the House is to be judged as done against our person and the whole Court of Parliament." The difference of rank between king and Parliament is still preserved, but it can now be symbolized through the relationship of head and members within one body; the composite representative has become "one body politic," the royal estate being enhanced by its participation in parliamentary representation, the Parliament by its participation in the majesty of royal representation.

The direction in which the symbols shift will have become clear from this passage: when articulation expands throughout society, the representative will also expand until the limit is reached where the membership of the society has become politically articulate down to the last individual, and, correspondingly, the society becomes the representative of itself. Symbolically this limit is reached with the masterful, dialectical concentration of Lincoln's "government of the people, by the people, for the people." The symbol "people" in this formula means successively the articulated political society, its representative, and the membership that is bound by the acts of the representative. The unsurpassable fusion of democratic symbolism with theoretical content in this formula is the secret of its effectiveness. The historical process in which the limit of articulation is reached that expresses itself in the symbolism of the "people" will occupy us in greater detail in a later part of these lectures. For the present it should be noted that the transition to the dialectical limit presupposes an articulation of society down to the individual as a representable unit. This peculiar type of articulation does not occur everywhere; in fact, it occurs only in Western societies. It is by far not an appurtenance of the nature of man but cannot be separated from certain historical conditions which again are given only in the Occident. In the Orient, where the specific conditions are historically not present, this type of articulation does not occur at all—and the Orient is the larger part of mankind.

6

Articulation, thus, is the condition of representation. In order to come into existence, a society must articulate itself by producing a representative that will act for it. The clarification of these concepts can now be continued. Behind the symbol "articulation" there hides nothing less than the historical process in which political societies, the nations, the empires, rise and fall, as well as the evolutions and revolutions between the two terminal points. This process is historically not so individualized for each instance of a political society that it would be impossible to bring the manifold of varieties under a few general types. But this is a vast topic (Toynbee has already filled six volumes with its exposition), and it must be set aside. The present concern will rather be whether the implications of the concept of articulation can be differentiated still further. This can, indeed, be done, and there exist several interesting attempts at further theoretization. In the nature of the case such attempts will be made when the articulation of a society has arrived at a critical juncture; the problem will attract attention when a society is about to come into existence, when it is about to disintegrate, or when it is in an epochal phase of its career. Such an epochal phase in the growth of Western societies occurred about the middle of the fifteenth century with the consolidation of the Western national realms after the Hundred Years' War. At this critical epoch one of the finest English political thinkers, Sir John Fortescue, tried to theorize the problem of articulation. It will be worth while to examine what he had to say. The political reality that interested Fortescue primarily was the kingdoms of England and France. His beloved England was a *dominium politicum et regale*, what today would be called a constitutional government; the bad France of Louis XI was a *dominium tantum regale*, something like a tyranny—good only for exile when the constitutional paradise became too inhospitable.[7] It was the merit, now, of Fortescue not to have stopped at a static description of the two types of government. To be sure, he used the static analogy of the organism when he insisted that a realm must have a ruler like a body a head, but then, in a brilliant page of his *De laudibus legum Anglie*, he made the analogy dynamic by comparing the creation of a realm with the growth of the articulate body out of the embryo.[8] A politically inarticulate social state breaks out into the articulation of the realm, *ex populo erumpit regnum*. Fortescue coined the term "eruption" as a technical term for designating the initial articulation of a society, and he coined the further term "proruption" for designating advances of articulation, such as the transition from a merely royal to a political realm. This theory of the eruption of a people is not a theory of a state of nature from which a people through contract will emerge into order under law. Fortescue was keenly aware of the difference. In order to make his point clear, he criticized St. Augustine's definition of the people as a multitude associated through consent to a right order and a communion of interests. Such a people, Fortescue insisted, would be *acephalus*, headless, the trunk of a body without a head; a realm will be

7. Fortescue, *The Governance of England*, ed. Plummer (Oxford, 1885), chaps. i and ii.

8. Fortescue, *De laudibus legum Anglie*, ed. S. B. Chrimes (Cambridge, 1942), chap. xiii.

achieved only when a head is erected, *rex erectus est*, that will rule the body.

To have created the concepts of eruption and proruption is no mean theoretical achievement in itself, because it allows us to distinguish the component in representation that is almost forgotten wherever the legal symbolism of the following centuries came to predominate in the interpretation of political reality. But Fortescue went even further. He understood that the organic analogy could be a scaffold for building his concept of eruption but that otherwise it was of little cognitive use. There was something about an articulated realm, an inner substance that provided the binding force of society, and this something could not be grasped by organic analogy. In order to come closer to this mysterious substance, he transferred the Christian symbol of the *corpus mysticum* to the realm. This was a momentous step in his analysis, of interest in more than one respect. In the first place, the fact that it could be taken at all was symptomatic of the decline of the Christian society, articulated into church and empire; and it was symptomatic, correspondingly, of the increasing consolidation of the national realms, of their closure as self-centered societies. The step indicated, second, that the realms had acquired a peculiar ultimacy of meaning. In the transfer of the *corpus mysticum* to the realm we can sense the evolution toward a type of political society that will succeed not only to the empire but also to the church. To be sure, these implications were not envisaged by Fortescue even vaguely; but the transfer, nevertheless, pointed toward a representative who will represent the society with regard to the whole range of human existence, including its spiritual dimension. Fortescue himself, on the contrary, was rather aware that the realm could even be called a *corpus mysticum* only analogically. The *tertium comparationis* would be the sacramental bond of the community, but the sacramental bond would be neither the Logos of Christ that lives in the members of the Christian *corpus mysticum* nor a perverted Logos as it lives in modern totalitarian communities. Nevertheless, while he was not clear about the implications of his search for an immanent Logos of society, he found a name for it; he called it the *intencio populi*. This *intencio populi* is the center of the mystical body of the realm; again in an organic analogy he described it as the heart from which is transmitted into the head and members of the body as its nourishing blood stream the political provision for the well-being of the people. Please note the function of the organic analogy in this context; it does not serve the identification of some member of a society with a corresponding organ of the body, but, on the contrary, it strives to show that the animating center of a social body is not to be found in any of its human members. The *intencio populi* is located neither in the royal representative nor in the people as a multitude of subjects but is the intangible living center of the realm as a whole. The word "people" in this formula does not signify an external multitude of human beings but the mystical substance erupting in articulation; and the word "intention" signifies the urge or drive of this substance to erupt and to maintain itself in articulate existence as an entity which, by means of its articulation, can provide for its well-being.

When Fortescue applied his conception concretely, in *The Governance of England*, he clarified his idea of the royal representative a bit further by contrasting it with the feudal, hierarchical conception of the royal estate. In the feudal conception the king was "the highest temporal estate on the earth," lower in rank than the ecclesiastical estate, but higher than the feudatories within the realm.[9] Fortescue accepted the order of estates in the *Christianitas;* he was far from conceiving the idea of a sovereign closed state; but he intruded the new *corpus mysticum* into the mystical body of Christ by attributing

9. Fortescue, *The Governance of England*, chap. viii.

a double function to the royal representative. In the order of the *Christianitas* the king remained the highest temporal estate, but, at the same time, the estate royal was to be understood as an office that ministers defense and justice to the realm. Fortescue quotes St. Thomas: "The king is given for the realm, and not the realm for the king"; and then he goes on to conclude: the king is in his realm what the pope is in the church, a *servus servorum Dei;* and, as a consequence, "all that the king does ought to be referred to his kingdom"—the most concentrated formulation of the problem of representation.[10]

7

The elaboration of this symbolism was Fortescue's personal achievement as a theorist. The realms of England and France impressed the age convincingly with their existence as power units once the Hundred Years' War had disentangled the feudal power field and resulted in the territorial fixation of the realms. Fortescue tried to clarify what these curious new entities, the realms, really were; and his theory was the original solution of a problem that presented itself in reality. In his solution he was aided, however, by a tradition of political articulation that had survived into his age from the period of the Great Migration, preceding the foundation of the Western empire. In a not sufficiently observed section of the *Governance of England* he used as his model of political articulation one of the many versions of the foundation of the migration kingdoms by a group of Trojan refugees. The myth of the foundation of Western kingdoms by a band of Trojans under the leadership of a son or grandson of Aeneas was fairly widespread; and, in the early Western centuries, it served the purpose of arrogating to the new establishments a dignity of foundation, of the same rank as the Roman. In Fortescue's model it was such a band under Brutus, the eponymos of the

10. *Ibid.*

Britains, which stood at the beginning of the world for England. When such a "great commonalty," he writes, "as was the fellowship that came into this land with Brute [was] willing to be unite and made a body politic called a realm, having a head to govern it . . . they chose the same Brute to be their head and king. And they and he upon this incorporation, institution, and uniting of themselves into a realm, ordained the same realm to be ruled and justified by such laws as they all would assent to."[11]

The Trojan component of the myth, the rivalry with Rome, is only of secondary interest for the present purpose; but under the guise of the myth there is recorded the actual articulation of migration bands into political societies. The myth points toward the initial phase of articulation itself, and it suggests a brief glance at the original accounts of such foundations as well as at the terminology in which the articulation is described. I shall select for this purpose a few passages from the *History of the Lombards* of Paulus Diaconus, written in the second half of the eighth century.

In the account of Paul the active history of the Lombards begins when, after the death of two dukes, the people decided that they no longer wanted to live in small federated groups under dukes and "set themselves a king like the other nations."[12] The language is influenced by the Israelitic desire, in the Book of Samuel, for a king like the other nations, but the actual process of the articulation of tribes into a realm is recorded quite clearly. When in the course of the migration the loose tribal federation proved too weak, a king was elected for the purpose of a more effective military and administrative conduct of affairs; and this king was selected from a family "which was considered among them particularly noble." The account reaches down to the historically

11. *Ibid.*, chap. 3; also *De laudibus*, chap. xiii.
12. *Pauli Historia Langobardorum* (Hanover, 1878), I, 14.

concrete, initial articulation. In this situation there was present what may be called a social raw material, consisting of groupings on the tribal level, homogeneous enough to articulate themselves into a larger society. There can be discerned, furthermore, a pressure of circumstances, providing the stimulus for articulation; and, finally, there were members of the group sufficiently distinguished by blood charisma and personal charisma to have become successful representatives.

But let us now follow the historian of the Lombards a bit further. Subsequent to the election of a king the victorious wars began. First the Herules were defeated and their power broken to the degree that "they no longer had a king."[13] Then followed the war with the Gepids, the decisive event being the death of the son of the Gepid king "who had been mainly instrumental in bringing the war about."[14] After the death of the young prince the Gepids fled, and, again, they "finally sank so deep that they no longer had a king." Similar passages could be accumulated from other historians of the migration period. Let us give just one good example: Isidorus tells how the Alans and Suebes lost the independence of their kingdom through the Goths but, oddly enough, preserved their kingship in Spain for a long time, "though they had no need for it in their undisturbed quiet." Throughout the historiography of the migration, from the fifth to the eighth centuries, the historical existence of a political society was consistently expressed in terms of acquisition, possession, or loss of the *rex*, of the royal representative. To be articulate for action meant to have a king; to lose the king meant to lose fitness for action; when the group did not act, it did not need a king.[15]

13. *Ibid.*, p. 20.

14. *Ibid.*, p. 23.

15. For a survey of the problem see Alfred Dove, *Der Wiederintritt des nationalen Prinzips in die Weltgeschichte* (1890) (in *Ausgewählte Schriften* [1898]).

8

The theoretizations just examined belonged to the period of foundation and to the late medieval consolidation of the Western political societies. The problem of representative articulation became of absorbing interest again when a society moved into the danger zone of disintegration. The malaise of the Third Republic was the climate in which Maurice Hauriou developed his theory of representation. I shall give a brief summary of the theory as it was developed by Hauriou in his *Précis de droit constitutionnel*.[16]

The power of a government is legitimate, according to Hauriou, by virtue of its functioning as the representative of an institution, specifically of the state. The state is a national community in which the ruling power conducts the business of the *res publica*. The first task of a ruling power is the creation of a politically unified nation by transforming the preexistent, unorganized manifold into a body organized for action. The nucleus of such an institution will be the idea, the *idée directrice*, of realizing and expanding it and of increasing its power; and the specific function of a ruler is the conception of this idea and its realization in history. The institution is successfully perfected when the ruler has become subordinate to the idea and when at the same time the *consentement coutumier* of the members is achieved. To be a representative means to guide, in a ruling position, the work of realizing the idea through institutional embodiment; and the power of a ruler has authority in so far as he is able to make his factual power representative of the idea.

From this conception Hauriou then derives a set of propositions concerning the relations between power and law: (1) The authority of a representative power precedes existentially the regulation of this power by positive law. (2) Power itself

16. Maurice Hauriou, *Précis de droit constitutionnel* (2d ed., 1929).

is a phenomenon of law by virtue of its basis in the institution; in so far as a power has representative authority, it can make positive law. (3) The origin of law cannot be found in legal regulations but must be sought in the decision which replaces a litigious situation by ordered power.

The theory just summarized as well as the set of propositions were pointed against certain well-known weaknesses of the Third Republic; the lesson of Hauriou's analysis may be concentrated in the thesis: In order to be representative, it is not enough for a government to be representative in the constitutional sense (our elemental type of representative institutions); it must also be representative in the existential sense of realizing the idea of the institution. And the implied warning may be explicated in the thesis: If a government is nothing but representative in the constitutional sense, a representative ruler in the existential sense will sooner or later make an end of it; and quite possibly the new existential ruler will not be too representative in the constitutional sense.

9

The analysis of representation on this level has come to its end. The summary of results can be brief.

We dealt successively with representation in the elemental and the existential sense. The transition from the one type to the other was necessary because the mere description of external realization of a political society did not touch the fundamental question of its existence. The inquiry into the conditions of existence, then, led to the problems of articulation as well as to an understanding of the close correspondence between types of articulation and representation. The result of this analysis can be expressed by the definition that a political society comes into existence when it articulates itself and produces a representative. If this definition be accepted, it follows that the elemental type of representative institutions covers only the external realization of one special type of articulation and representation. In critical science it will, therefore, be advisable to restrict the use of the term "representation" to its existential sense. Only when its use is restricted in this manner will social articulation come into clear view as the existentially overriding problem; and only then will there be gained a clear understanding of the very special historical conditions under which the conventionally so-called representative institutions can develop. It was hinted already that they occur in the Greco-Roman and Western civilizations only; and the condition of their development was formulated in a preliminary fashion as the articulation of the individual as a representable unit. Incidental to the analysis, then, emerged a number of problems that could not be pursued further at the moment—such as the symbol of the "people," Fortescue's *intencio populi* with its immanentist implications, and the relation of such a closed realm to the spiritual representation of man in the church. These loose ends will be gathered up in the later course of these lectures.

The adequate differentiation of concepts, however, proved to be not merely a matter of theoretical concern. The insufficient distinction between elemental and existential problems could be observed as a fact in political reality. As an occurrence in reality this confusion raises a problem of its own. The persistent arrogation of the symbol "representation" for a special type of articulation is a symptom of political and civilizational provincialism. And provincialisms of this kind, when they obscure the structure of reality, may become dangerous. Hauriou very strongly suggested that representation in the elemental sense is no insurance against existential disintegration and rearticulation of a society. When a representative does not fulfil his existential task, no constitutional legality of his position will save him; when a creative minority, in Toynbee's language, has become a dominant minority, it is in danger of being replaced by a new creative minority. The practical disregard for this problem has been an important contributive factor in our time in the serious internal upheavals of Western political societies as well as in their tremendous international repercussions. Our own foreign policy was a factor in aggravating international disorder through its sincere but naïve endeavor of curing the evils of the world by spreading representative institutions in the elemental sense to areas where the existential conditions for their functioning were not given. Such provincialism, persistent in the face of its consequences, is in itself an interesting problem for the scientist. One cannot explain the odd policies of Western democratic powers leading to continuous warfare, with weaknesses of individual statesmen—though such weaknesses are strongly in evidence. They are rather symptomatic of a massive resistance to face reality, deeply rooted in the sentiments and opinion of the broad masses of our contemporary Western societies. Only because they are symptoms of a mass phenomenon is it justified to speak of a crisis of Western civilization. The causes of this phenomenon will receive careful attention in the course of these lectures; but their critical exploration presupposes a clearer understanding of the relation between theory and reality. We must, therefore, resume the description of the theoretical situation that was left incomplete at the opening of the present lecture.

II

REPRESENTATION AND TRUTH

✻

1

IN A first approach, the analysis used the Aristotelian method of examining language symbols as they occur in political reality, in the hope that the procedure of clarification would lead to critically tenable concepts. Society was a cosmion of meaning, illuminated from within by its own self-interpretation; and, since this little world of meaning was precisely the object to be explored by political science, the method of starting from the symbols in reality seemed at least to assure the grip on the object.

To assure the object, however, is no more than a first step in an inquiry, and before venturing further on the way it must be ascertained whether there is a way at all and where it leads. A number of assumptions were made that cannot remain unchallenged. It was taken for granted that one could speak of social reality and of a theorist who explored it; of critical clarification and theoretical contexts; of symbols of theory which did not seem to be symbols in reality; and of concepts which referred *to* reality while, at the same time, their meaning was derived *from* reality through the mysterious critical clarification. Obviously a whole series of questions imposes itself. Is it possible that a theorist be a person outside social reality, or is he not rather a part of it? And if he be himself a part of reality, in what sense can this reality be his object? And what does he actually do when he clarifies the symbols which occur in reality? If he does no more than introduce distinctions, remove equivocations, extract a true core from propositions that were too sweeping, make symbols and propositions logically consistent, etc., would then not everybody who participates in the self-interpretation of society be at least a tentative theorist, and would theory in a technical sense be anything but a better reflected self-interpretation? Or does the theorist perhaps possess standards of interpretation of his own by which he measures the self-interpretation of society, and does clarification mean that he develops an interpretation of superior quality on occasion of the symbols in reality? And, if this should be the case, will there not arise a conflict between two interpretations?

The symbols in which a society interprets the meaning of its existence are meant to be true; if the theorist arrives at a different interpretation, he arrives at a different truth concerning the meaning of human existence in society. And then one would have to inquire: What is this truth that is represented by the theorist, this truth that furnishes him with standards by which he can measure the truth represented by society? What is the source of this truth that apparently is developed in critical opposition to society? And if the truth represented by the theorist should be different from the truth represented by society, how can the one be developed out of the other by something that looks as innocuous as a critical clarification?

2

Certainly these questions cannot be answered all at once; but the catalogue should indicate the complexities of the theoretical situation. The analysis will suitably concentrate on the point where the catalogue apparently comes closest to the present topic, that is, in the questions concerning a conflict of truth. A truth represented by the theorist was opposed to another truth represented by society. Is such language empty, or is there really something like a representation of truth to be found in political societies in history? If this should be the case, the problem of representation would not be exhausted by representation in the existential sense. It would then become necessary to distinguish between the representation of society by its articulated representatives and a second relation in which society itself becomes the representative of something beyond itself, of a transcendent reality. Is such a relation to be found concretely in historical societies?

As a matter of fact, this relation is to be found as far back as the recorded history of major political societies beyond the tribal level goes. All the early empires, Near Eastern as well as Far Eastern, understood themselves as representatives of a transcendent order, of the order of the cosmos; and some of them even understood this order as a "truth." Whether one turns to the earliest Chinese sources in the *Shû King* or to the inscriptions of Egypt, Babylonia, Assyria, or Persia, one uniformly finds the order of the empire interpreted as a representation of cosmic order in the medium of human society. The empire is a cosmic analogue, a little world reflecting the order of the great, comprehensive world. Rulership becomes the task of securing the order of society in harmony with cosmic order; the territory of the empire is an analogical representation of the world with its four quarters; the great ceremonies of the empire represent the rhythm of the cosmos; festivals and sacrifices are a cosmic liturgy, a symbolic participation of the cosmion in the cosmos; and the ruler himself represents the society, because on earth he represents the transcendent power which maintains cosmic order. The term "cosmion," thus, gains a new component of meaning as the representative of the cosmos.

Inevitably such an enterprise of representative order is exposed to resistance from enemies within and without; and the ruler is no more than a human being and may fail through circumstance or mismanagement, with the result of internal revolutions and external defeats. The experience of resistance, of possible or actual defeat now, is the occasion on which the meaning of truth comes into clearer view. In so far as the order of society does not exist automatically but must be founded, preserved, and defended, those who are on the side of order represent the truth, while their enemies represent disorder and falsehood.

This level of self-interpretation of an empire was reached by the Achaemenides. In the Behistun Inscription, celebrating the feats of Darius I, the king was victorious because he was the righteous tool of Ahuramazda; he "was not wicked, nor a liar"; neither he nor his family were servants of Ahriman, of the Lie, but "ruled according to righteousness."[1] With regard to the enemies, on the other hand, the inscription assures us that "lies made them revolt, so that they deceived the people. Then Ahuramazda delivered them into my hand."[2] The expansion of empire and the submission of its enemies become, in this conception, the establishment of a terrestrial realm of peace, through the king who acts as the representative of the divine Lord of Wisdom. Moreover, the conception has its ramifications into the ethos of political conduct. The rebels against Truth, to be sure, are recognizable as such by their resistance to the king, but they also are recognizable as representatives of the Lie by the propaganda lies which they spread in order to deceive the people. On the king, on the other hand, is incumbent the duty of being scrupulously correct in his own pronouncements. The Behistun Inscription contains the touching passage: "By the grace of Ahuramazda there is also much else that has been done by me which is not graven in this inscription; it has not been inscribed lest he who should read this inscription hereafter should then hold that which has been done by me to be too much and should not believe it, but

1. L. W. King and R. C. Thompson, *The Sculptures and Inscriptions of Darius the Great on the Rock of Behistun* (London, 1907), § LXIII, p. 72.

2. *Ibid.*, § LIV, p. 65.

should take it to be lies."[3] No fibs for a representative of the truth; he must even lean over backward.

When faced with such ostentatiously virtuous conduct, one begins to wonder what the other side would have to say if it had a chance to talk back. And one would like to know what sort of amenities would be exchanged when two or more such representatives of truth were to become competitors in establishing the one true order of mankind. In the nature of the case, such clashes are rare; nevertheless, there occurred a fine instance on occasion of the Mongol expansion which, in the thirteenth century, threatened the Western Empire with extinction. Both the pope and the king of France sent embassies to the Mongol court in order to feel out the intentions of the dangerous conquerors and generally to form contacts; the notes carried by the ambassadors, as well as their oral presentations, must have contained complaints about the Mongol massacres in eastern Europe, suggestions concerning the immorality of such conduct, especially when the victims were Christians, and even the request that the Mongols should receive baptism and submit to the authority of the pope. The Mongols, however, turned out to be masters of political theology. There is preserved a letter from Kuyuk Khan to Innocent IV, in which the presentations of the ambassadors are carefully answered. Let me quote a passage:

> You have said it would be good if I received baptism;
> You have informed me of it, and you have sent me the request.
> This your request, we do not understand it.
>
> Another point: You have sent me these words "You have taken
> all the realms of the Magyars and the Christians altogether; I
> am surprised at that. Tell us what has been the fault of these?"
> These your words we did not understand them.
>
> (In order to avoid, however, any appearance that we pass over
> this point in silence, we speak in answer to you thus:)

3. *Ibid.*, § LVIII, p. 68.

The Order of God, both Genghis Khan and the Kha Khan have
  sent it to make it known,
But the Order of God they did not believe.
Those of whom you speak did even meet in a great council,
They showed themselves arrogant and have killed our envoy-
  ambassadors.
The eternal God has killed and destroyed the men in those
  realms.
Save by order of God, anybody by his own force, how could he
  kill, how could he take?
And if you say: "I am a Christian; I adore God; I despise the
  others,"
How shall you know whom God forgives and to whom He grants
  His mercy?
How do you know that you speak such words?

By the virtue of God,
From the rising of the sun to its setting,
All realms have been granted to us.

Without the Order of God
How could anyone do anything?

Now, you ought to say from a sincere heart:
"We shall be your subjects;
We shall give unto you our strength."
You in person, at the head of the kings, all together, without ex-
  ception, come and offer us service and homage;
Then shall we recognize your submission.
And if you do not observe the Order of God,
And disobey our orders,
We shall know you to be our enemies.

That is what we make known to you.
If you disobey,
What shall we know then?
God will know it.[4]

4. The Persian original and a French translation of this letter are to be found in
Paul Pelliot, *Les Mongols et la papauté* ("Revue de l'Orient Chrétien," 3ᵉ série, Vol. III
[1923]). The passage in parentheses is taken from a Latin version of the same letter,

This meeting of truth with truth has a familiar ring. And the ring will become even more familiar when a few corollaries of Mongol legal theory are taken into account. The Order of God on which the imperial construction was based is preserved in the edicts of Kuyuk Khan and Mangu Khan:

By order of the living God
Genghis Khan, the sweet and venerable Son of God, says:
God is high above all, He, Himself, the immortal God,
And on earth, Genghis Khan is the only Lord.[5]

The empire of the Lord Genghis Khan is *de jure* in existence even if it is not yet realized *de facto*. All human societies are part of the Mongol empire by virtue of the Order of God, even if they are not yet conquered. The actual expansion of the empire, therefore, follows a very strict process of law. Societies whose turn for actual integration into the empire has come must be notified by ambassadors of the Order of God and requested to make their submission. If they refuse, or perhaps kill the ambassadors, then they are rebels, and military sanctions will be taken against them. The Mongol empire, thus, by its own legal order has never conducted a war but only punitive expeditions against rebellious subjects of the empire.[6]

It will have become clear by now that the Behistun Inscription and the Mongol Orders are not oddities of a remote past but instances of a structure in politics that may occur at any time, and especially in our own. The self-understanding of a society as the representative of cosmic order originates in the period of the cosmological empires in the technical sense, but

---

published in *Cronica Fratris Salimbene*, ed. O. Holder-Egger, *MGH, SS*, XXXII, 208. The extant Mongol documents are collected and edited in Eric Voegelin, *The Mongol Orders of Submission to European Powers, 1245–1255* ("Byzantion," Vol. XI [1941]).

5. From the Edict of Kuyuk Khan in Vincent of Beauvais, *Speculum historiale* (*s.l.*, 1474), Book XXXI, chaps. 51, 52; Voegelin, *op. cit.*, p. 389.

6. Voegelin, *op. cit.*, pp. 404 ff.

it is not confined to this period. Not only does cosmological representation survive in the imperial symbols of the Western Middle Ages or in continuity into the China of the twentieth century; its principle is also recognizable where the truth to be represented is symbolized in an entirely different manner. In Marxian dialectics, for instance, the truth of cosmic order is replaced by the truth of a historically immanent order. Nevertheless, the Communist movement is a representative of this differently symbolized truth in the same sense in which a Mongol Khan was the representative of the truth contained in the Order of God; and the consciousness of this representation leads to the same political and legal constructions as in the other instances of imperial representation of truth. Its order is in harmony with the truth of history; its aim is the establishment of the realm of freedom and peace; the opponents run counter to the truth of history and will be defeated in the end; nobody can be at war with the Soviet Union legitimately but must be a representative of untruth in history, or, in contemporary language, an aggressor; and the victims are not conquered but liberated from their oppressors and therewith from the untruth of their existence.

3

Political societies as representatives of truth, thus, actually occur in history. But as soon as the fact is recognized new questions impose themselves. Are all political societies monadic entities, expressing the universality of truth by their universal claim of empire? Can the monadism of such representation not be broken by questioning the validity of the truth in each case? Is the clash of empires the only test of truth, with the result that the victorious power is right? Obviously, the mere raising of these questions is in part the answer. In the very act of raising them the spell of monadic representation is broken; with our questioning we have set up ourselves as the representatives of the truth in whose name we are questioning—even though its nature and source should be only dimly discerned. Beyond this point, however, the difficulties begin. The challenge to imperial truth and the establishment of the challenging theoretical truth are a rather complex affair requiring a more detailed examination.

The discovery of the truth that is apt to challenge the truth of the cosmological empires is itself a historical event of major dimensions. It is a process which occupies about five centuries in the history of mankind, that is, roughly the period from 800 to 300 B.C.; it occurs simultaneously in the various civilizations but without apparent mutual influences. In China it is the age of Confucius and Lao-tse as well as of the other philosophical schools; in India, the age of the *Upanishads* and the Buddha; in Persia, of Zoroastrianism; in Israel, of the Prophets; in Hellas, of the philosophers and of tragedy. As a specifically characteristic phase in this long-drawn-out process may be recognized the period around 500 B.c. when Heraclitus, the Buddha, and Confucius were contemporaries. This simultaneous outbreak of the truth of the mystic philosophers and prophets has attracted the attention of historians and philosophers ever since it came into full view with the enlargement of the historical horizon in the eighteenth and nineteenth centuries. Some are inclined to recognize it as the decisive epoch in the history of mankind. Karl Jaspers, in a recent study on *Ursprung und Ziel der Geschichte*, has called it the axis time of human history, the one great epoch that is relevant for all mankind, as distinguished from the epoch of Christ which supposedly is relevant for Christians only.[7] And in the classic masterpiece of contemporary philosophy of society, in his *Les deux sources de la morale et de la religion*, Henri Bergson has formed the concepts of a closed and an open society for the

7. Karl Jaspers, *Ursprung und Ziel der Geschichte* (Zurich, 1949), pp. 18 ff.

purpose of characterizing the two social states in the development of mankind which are created by this epoch.[8] No more than such brief hints are possible for the general orientation of the problem; we must turn to the more special form which this outbreak has assumed in the West. Only in the West, owing to specific historical circumstances that were not present in other civilizations, has the outbreak culminated in the establishment of philosophy in the Greek sense and in particular of a theory of politics.

4

You are familiar with Plato's often-quoted phrase that a polis is man written large.[9] This formula, one may say, is the creed of the new epoch. To be sure, it is Plato's first word in the matter and by far not his last. But, however much this principle must be limited by the introduction of other ones, and even though concessions must be made to cosmological interpretation and to the truth which, after all, it contains, this is the dynamic core of the new theory. The wedge of this principle must be permanently driven into the idea that society represents nothing but cosmic truth, today quite as much as in the time of Plato. A political society in existence will have to be an ordered cosmion, but not at the price of man; it should be not only a microcosmos but also a macroanthropos. This principle of Plato will briefly be referred to as the anthropological principle.

Two aspects of the principle must be distinguished. Under the first aspect it is a general principle for the interpretation of society; under a second aspect it is an instrument of social critique.

As a general principle it means that in its order every society

8. Henri Bergson, *Les deux sources de la morale et de la religion* (Paris, 1932), *passim*, esp. pp. 287 ff.

9. Plato *Republic* 368c–d.

reflects the type of men of whom it is composed. One would have to say, for instance, that cosmological empires consist of a type of men who experience the truth of their existence as a harmony with the cosmos. That in itself is, of course, a heuristic principle of the first importance; whenever the theorist wants to understand a political society, it will be one of his first tasks, if not the very first, to ascertain the human type which expresses itself in the order of this concrete society. Plato used his principle under this first aspect when he described the Athenian society in which he lived as the sophist written large, explaining the peculiarities of Athenian order by referring them to the socially predominant sophistic type;[10] he, furthermore, used it in this sense when he developed his Polis of the Idea as the paradigmatic construction of a social order in which should find expression his philosophical type of man;[11] and he, finally, used it under this first aspect when in *Republic* viii–ix he interpreted the successive changes of political order as the expression of corresponding changes in the socially predominant human types.[12]

Inseparably connected with this first aspect is the use of the principle as an instrument of social critique. That differences of social order come into view as differences of human types at all is due to the discovery of a true order of the human psyche and to the desire of expressing the true order in the social environment of the discoverer. Now, truth is never discovered in empty space; the discovery is a differentiating act in a tightly packed environment of opinion; and, if the discovery concerns the truth of human existence, it will shock the environment in its strongest convictions on a broad front. As soon as the discoverer begins to communicate, to invite acceptance, to persuade, he will inevitably run into a resistance that may prove fatal, as in the case of Socrates. Just as in the cosmological em-

10. *Ibid.* 492b.   11. *Ibid.* 435e.   12. *Ibid.* 544d–e.

pires the enemy is discovered as the representative of the Lie, so is now, through the experience of resistance and conflict, the opponent discovered as the representative of untruth, of falsehood, of the *pseudos*,[13] with regard to the order of the soul. Hence, the several Platonic types do not form a flat catalogue of human varieties but are distinguished as the one type of true humanity and the several types of disorder in the psyche. The true type is the philosopher, while the sophist becomes the prototype of disorder.[14]

The identification of the true type with the philosopher is a point that must be well understood, because today its meaning is obscured by modernistic prejudices. Today, in the retrospect of a history of philosophy, Plato's philosophy has become one among others. In Plato's intention, his theory did not develop *a* philosophy of man; Plato was engaged concretely in the exploration of the human soul, and the true order of the soul turned out to be dependent on philosophy in the strict sense of the love of the divine *sophon*.[15] It is the meaning that was still alive in St. Augustine when he translated the Greek philosopher into his Latin as the *amator sapientiae*.[16] The truth of the soul would be achieved through its loving orientation toward the *sophon*. The true order of man, thus, is a constitution of the soul, to be defined in terms of certain experiences which have become predominant to the point of forming a character. The true order of the soul in this sense furnishes the standard for measuring and classifying the empirical variety of human types as well as of the social order in which they find their expression.

13. *Ibid.* 382a.

14. *Philosophos* and *philodoxos* distinguished (*ibid.* 480).

15. Plato *Phaedrus* 278d–e; cf. the complex of Heraclitean fragments B 35, B 40, B 50, B 108.

16. St. Augustine *Civitas Dei* viii. 1.

5

This is the crucial point on which the meaning of theory depends. Theory is not just any opining about human existence in society; it rather is an attempt at formulating the meaning of existence by explicating the content of a definite class of experiences. Its argument is not arbitrary but derives its validity from the aggregate of experiences to which it must permanently refer for empirical control. Aristotle was the first thinker to recognize this condition of theorizing about man. He coined a term for the man whose character is formed by the aggregate of experiences in question, and he called him the *spoudaios*, the mature man.[17] The *spoudaios* is the man who has maximally actualized the potentialities of human nature, who has formed his character into habitual actualization of the dianoetic and ethical virtues, the man who at the fullest of his development is capable of the *bios theoretikos*. Hence, the science of ethics in the Aristotelian sense is a type study of the *spoudaios*.[18] Moreover, Aristotle was acutely aware of the practical corollaries of such a theory of man. In the first place, theory cannot be developed under all conditions by everybody. The theorist need perhaps not be a paragon of virtue himself, but he must, at least, be capable of imaginative re-enactment of the experiences of which theory is an explication; and this faculty can be developed only under certain conditions such as inclination, an economic basis that will allow the investment of years of work into such studies, and a social environment which does not suppress a man when he engages in them. And, second, theory as an explication of certain experiences is intelligible only to those in whom the explication will stir up parallel experiences as the empirical basis for testing the truth of theory. Unless a theoretical exposition activates the cor-

17. Aristotle *Nicomachean Ethics* 1113a, 29–35.
18. *Ibid.* 1176a, 17 ff.

responding experiences at least to a degree, it will create the impression of empty talk or will perhaps be rejected as an irrelevant expression of subjective opinions. A theoretical debate can be conducted only among *spoudaioi* in the Aristotelian sense; theory has no argument against a man who feels, or pretends to feel, unable of re-enacting the experience. Historically, as a consequence, the discovery of theoretical truth may not at all find acceptance in the surrounding society. Aristotle had no illusions on this point. To be sure, like Plato, he attempted a paradigmatic construction of a social order that would express the truth of the *spoudaios*, in *Politics* vii–viii; but he also asserted with firm regret that in none of the Hellenic poleis of his time could there be found a hundred men who were able to form the ruling nucleus of such a society; any attempt at realizing it would be utterly futile. A practical impasse seems to be the result.[19]

A study of the experiences is impossible in the present context. In view of the vastness of the subject, even a lengthy sketch would be pitiably inadequate. No more than a brief catalogue can be given that will appeal to your historical knowledge. To the previously mentioned love of the *sophon* may now be added the variants of the Platonic Eros toward the *kalon* and the *agathon*, as well as the Platonic Dike, the virtue of right superordination and subordination of the forces in the soul, in opposition to the sophistic *polypragmosyne;* and, above all, there must be included the experience of Thanatos, of death, as the cathartic experience of the soul which purifies conduct by placing it into the longest of all long-range perspectives, into the perspective of death. Under the aspect of death the life of the philosophical man becomes for Plato the practice of dying; the philosophers' souls are dead souls—in the sense of the *Gorgias*—and, when the philosopher speaks as the representative of truth, he does it with the authority of

19. Aristotle *Politics* 1286b, 8–21 and 1302a, 2.

death over the shortsightedness of life. To the three fundamental forces of Thanatos, Eros, and Dike should be added,
still within the Platonic range, the experiences in which the
inner dimension of the soul is given in height and depth. The
dimension in height is scaled through the mystical ascent,
over the *via negativa*, toward the border of transcendence—the
subject of the *Symposion*. The dimension in depth is probed
through the anamnetic descent into the unconscious, into the
depth from where are drawn up the "true logoi" of the
Timaeus and *Critias*.

The discovery and exploration of these experiences started
centuries before Plato a.d continued after him. The Platonic
descent into the depth of the soul, for instance, differentiated
experiences that were explored by Heraclitus and Aeschylus.
And the name of Heraclitus reminds us that the Ephesian had
already discovered the triad of love, hope, and faith which re-
appeared in the experiential triad of St. Paul. For the *via
negativa* Plato could draw on the mysteries as well as on the
description of the way toward truth that Parmenides had
given in his didactic poem. And there should be mentioned, as
close to the Platonic range, the Aristotelian *philia*, the experiential nucleus of true community between mature men; and
again the Aristotelian love of the noetic self is hearkening
back to the Heraclitean followership of the common Logos of
mankind.

6

Brief and incomplete as these hints are, they should be sufficient to evoke the class of experiences which form the basis
of theory in the Platonic-Aristotelian sense. It must now be
ascertained why they should become the carriers of a truth
about human existence in rivalry with the truth of the older
myth, and why the theorist, as the representative of this truth,
should be able to pit his authority against the authority of
society.

The answer to this question must be sought in the nature of the experience under discussion. The discovery of the new truth is not an advancement of psychological knowledge in the immanentist sense; one would rather have to say that the psyche itself is found as a new center in man at which he experiences himself as open toward transcendental reality. Moreover, this center is not found as if it were an object that had been present all the time and only escaped notice. The psyche as the region in which transcendence is experienced must be differentiated out of a more compact structure of the soul; it must be developed and named. With due regard for the problem of compactness and differentiation, one might almost say that before the discovery of the psyche man had no soul. Hence, it is a discovery which produces its experiential material along with its explication; the openness of the soul is experienced through the opening of the soul itself. This opening, which is as much action as it is passion, we owe to the genius of the mystic philosophers.[20]

These experiences become the source of a new authority. Through the opening of the soul the philosopher finds himself in a new relation with God; he not only discovers his own psyche as the instrument for experiencing transcendence but at the same time discovers the divinity in its radically nonhuman transcendence. Hence, the differentiation of the psyche is inseparable from a new truth about God. The true order of the soul can become the standard for measuring both human types and types of social order because it represents the truth about human existence on the border of transcendence. The meaning of the anthropological principle must, therefore, be qualified by the understanding that not an arbitrary idea of man as a world-immanent being becomes the instrument of social

---

20. On the evolution of the meaning of psyche see Werner Jaeger, *The Theology of the Early Greek Philosophers* (Oxford, 1947), esp. chap. v; and Bruno Snell, *Die Entdeckung des Geistes: Studien zur Entstehung des europäischen Denkens bei den Griechen* (Hamburg, 1948).

critique but the idea of a man who has found his true nature through finding his true relation to God. The new measure that is found for the critique of society is, indeed, not man himself but man in so far as through the differentiation of his psyche he has become the representative of divine truth.

The anthropological principle, thus, must be supplemented by a second principle for the theoretical interpretation of society. Plato expressed it when he created his formula, "God is the Measure," in opposition to the Protagorean, "Man is the Measure."[21] In formulating this principle, Plato drew the sum of a long development. His ancestor Solon already had been in search of the truth that could be imposed with authority on the factions of Athens, and with a sigh he admitted: "It is very hard to know the unseen measure of right judgment; and yet it alone contains the right boundaries of all things."[22] As a statesman he lived in the tension between the unseen measure and the necessity of incarnating it in the eunomia of society; on the one hand: "The mind of the immortals is all unseen to men";[23] and, on the other hand: "At the behest of the gods have I done what I did."[24] Heraclitus, then, who always looms as the great shadow behind the ideas of Plato, went deeper into the experiences leading toward the invisible measure. He recognized its overruling validity: "The invisible harmony is better (or: greater, more powerful) than the visible."[25] But this invisible harmony is difficult to find, and it will not be found at all unless the soul be animated by an anticipating urge in the right direction: "If you do not hope you will not find the unhoped-for, since it is hard to be found and the way

21. Plato *Laws* 716c.

22. *Elegy and Iambus* ("Loeb Classical Library"), Vol. I, Solon 16.

23. *Ibid.*, Solon 17.

24. *Ibid.*, Solon 34, vs. 6.

25. Diels-Kranz, *Fragmente der Vorsokratiker* (5th ed.; Berlin, 1934-38), Heraclitus B 54.

is all but impassable,"[26] and: "Through lack of faith (*apistie*) the divine(?) escapes being known."[27] And, finally, Plato has absorbed the Xenophantic critique of unseemly symbolization of the gods. As long as men create gods in their image, is the argument of Xenophanes, the true nature of the one God who is "greatest among gods and men, not like mortals in body or thought," must remain hidden;[28] and only when the one God is understood in his formless transcendence as the same God for every man will the nature of every man be understood as the same by virtue of the sameness of his relation to the transcendent divinity. Of all the early Greek thinkers, Xenophanes had perhaps the clearest insight into the constitution of a universal idea of man through the experience of universal transcendence.[29]

The truth of man and the truth of God are inseparably one. Man will be in the truth of his existence when he has opened his psyche to the truth of God; and the truth of God will become manifest in history when it has formed the psyche of man into receptivity for the unseen measure. This is the great subject of the *Republic;* at the center of the dialogue Plato placed the Parable of the Cave, with its description of the *periagoge*, the conversion, the turning-around from the untruth of human existence as it prevailed in the Athenian sophistic society to the truth of the Idea.[30] Moreover, Plato understood that the best way of securing the truth of existence was proper education from early childhood; for that reason, in *Republic* ii, he wanted to remove unseemly symbolizations of the gods, as they were to be found in the poets, from the education of the young and have them replaced by seemly symbols.[31] On this

---

26. *Ibid.*, Heraclitus B 18.
27. *Ibid.*, Heraclitus B 86.
28. *Ibid.*, Xenophanes B 23.
29. Jaeger, *op. cit.*, chap. iii: "Xenophanes' Doctrine of God."
30. Plato *Republic* 518d–e.   31. *Ibid.* 378–79.

occasion he developed the technical vocabulary for dealing with such problems. In order to speak of the various types of symbolization, he coined the term "theology" and called them types of theology, *typoi peri theologias*.[32] On the same occasion Plato, furthermore, distinguished the gnoseological component of the problem. If the soul is exposed in its youth to the wrong type of theology, it will be warped at its decisive center where it knows about the nature of God; it will fall a prey to the "arch-lie," the *alethos pseudos*, of misconception about the gods.[33] This lie is not an ordinary lie in daily life for which there may be extenuating circumstances; it is the supreme lie of "ignorance, of *agnoia*, within the soul."[34] If now the Platonic terminology be adopted, one may say, therefore, that the anthropological principle in a theoretical interpretation of society requires the theological principle as its correlate. The validity of the standards developed by Plato and Aristotle depends on the conception of a man who can be the measure of society because God is the measure of his soul.

7

The theorist is the representative of a new truth in rivalry with the truth represented by society. So much is secured. But there seems to be left the difficulty of the impasse that the new truth has little chance of becoming socially effective, of forming a society in its image.

This impasse, in fact, did never exist. Its appearance was created through Plato's disappointment with Athens. The polis of his time was indeed no longer capable of a great spiritual reform—but the polis had not always been so sterile as it looks when attention is focused on its resistance to Socrates and Plato. The Platonic-Aristotelian elaboration of the new truth marked the end of a long history; it was the work of Athenian thinkers who hardly could have accomplished their

32. *Ibid.* 379a.   33. *Ibid.* 382a.   34. *Ibid.* 382b.

theoretical generalization without the preceding concrete practice of Athenian politics. The paradigmatic constructions of Plato and Aristotle would have appeared as odd fancies to their contemporaries unless the Athens of Marathon and the tragedy had been the living memory of an ephemeral representation of the new truth. Here, for a golden hour in history, the miracle had happened of a political society articulated down to the individual citizen as a representable unit, the miracle of a generation which individually experienced the responsibility of representing the truth of the soul and expressed this experience through the tragedy as a public cult. We must examine one such tragedy in order to understand the new type of representation; and the purpose will be served best by the *Suppliants* of Aeschylus.

The plot of the *Suppliants* turns on a legal problem and its solution through political action. The daughters of Danaus come with their father on their flight from Egypt to Argos because the sons of Aegyptus try to force them into an unwanted marriage. In Argos, the home of their ancester Io, they hope to find asylum. Pelasgus, the king of Argos, appears, and the case is presented to him by the fugitives. Immediately he sees the dilemma: either he must deny asylum and let the suppliants be taken by the Egyptians who are near in pursuit, and thereby incur the wrath of Zeus, or he will become involved in a war with the Egyptians that at best will be a costly affair for his polis. He states the alternatives: "Without harm I do not know how to help you; and yet again it is not advisable to slight such supplications." Frankly he describes himself as being in a state of perplexed indecision; his soul is gripped by fear whether "to act, or not to act and take what fortune brings."[35]

The decision is not easy. By the law, the *nomos* of their country, the damsels in distress have no case against the Egyp-

35. Aeschylus *Suppliants* v. 380.

tians who want them in marriage; but the suppliants are quick to remind the king that there is a higher justice, *dike*, that the marriage is offensive to them, and that Zeus is the god of suppliants. On the one side, the king is admonished to take Dike as his ally in deciding the case; on the other side, he must consider the interests of the Argivian polis. If he involves his city in a war, he will be charged with honoring aliens at the expense of his country; if he abandons the suppliants, his children and his house will have to pay measure for measure for this violation of Dike. Gravely he reflects: "There is need of deep and saving counsel, like a diver's, descending to the depths, with keen eye and not too much perturbed."[36] We are reminded of the Heraclitean "deep-knowing," of the conception of the soul whose border cannot be reached because its Logos is too deep.[37] The lines of Aeschylus translate the Heraclitean conception of depth into the action of descent.[38]

At this juncture, however, there enters the problem of constitutional government as a complicating factor. As far as the king himself is concerned, the descent brings the desired judgment in favor of the suppliants; but Pelasgus is a constitutional king, not a tyrant. The people, the *demos*, who will have to bear the burden of the inevitable war must be consulted and their consent reached. The king leaves the suppliants in order to assemble the people and to submit the case to the general body, the *koinon;* he will try to persuade them to agree with the decision which he has reached in his own soul. The speech of the prince is successful; the proper decrees, the *psephismata*, are passed unanimously. The people enter into the argument

36. *Ibid.* 407–8.

37. Diels-Kranz, *op. cit.*, Heraclitus B 45.

38. On the genesis of a conception of "depth" of the soul see Snell, *op. cit.*, esp. pp. 32 ff.

of the subtly winding speech, following the royal descent into the depth of the soul. The Peitho, the persuasion of the king, forms the souls of his listeners, who are willing to let themselves be formed, and makes the Dike of Zeus prevail against passion, so that the mature decision represents the truth of the God. The chorus summarizes the meaning of the event in the line: "It is Zeus who brings the end to pass."[39]

The tragedy was a public cult—and a very expensive one. It presupposed as its audience a people who would follow the performance with a keen sense of *tua res agitur*. They would have to understand the meaning of action, of drama, as action in obedience to Dike, and to consider the escape into the easy way out as nonaction. They would have to understand the Athenian *prostasia* as the organization of a people under a leader—in which the leader tries to represent the Jovian Dike and uses his power of persuasion to create the same state of the soul in the people on occasion of concrete decisions, while the people are willing to follow such persuasive leadership into the representation of truth, through action in battle against a demonically disordered world, symbolized in the *Suppliants* by the Egyptians. The tragedy in its great period is a liturgy which re-enacts the great decision for Dike. Even if the audience is not an assembly of heroes, the spectators must at least be disposed to regard tragic action as paradigmatic; the heroic soul-searching and suffering of consequences must be experienced as holding a valid appeal; the fate of the hero must arouse the shudder of his own fate in the soul of the spectator. The meaning of tragedy as a state cult consists in representative suffering.[40]

39. The analysis of the *Suppliants* in Erik Wolf, *Griechisches Rechtsdenken*, Vol. I: *Vorsokratiker und frühe Dichter* (Frankfurt a.M., 1950), pp. 345–56, was too recent to be used in the present lectures.

40. On representative suffering through descent to the depth see especially Aeschylus *Prometheus* 1026 ff.

8

The miracle of tragic Athens was short lived; its glory was submerged in the horrors of the Peloponnesian War. With the decline of Athens the problems of tragedy changed. In a late work of Euripides, in the *Troades* of *ca.* 415, the issue is the mass of filth, abuse, vulgarity, and atrocity displayed by the Greeks on occasion of the fall of Troy; the heroic adventure slides into a morass that will suck down the Greeks themselves. Ominous is the opening scene, the conversation between Athena and Poseidon; Athena, who formerly protected the Greeks, will now switch sides because her temple has been insulted and combine with Poseidon for the destruction of the victors on their homeward trip. The tragedy falls into the year after the butchery at Melos which revealed the corruption of Athenian ethos, as we know it from Thucydides' unforgettable Melian dialogue; and it falls into the very year of the Sicilian expedition that was to end disastrously. It was the year in which the doom of Athens was sealed; the gods, indeed, had switched sides.[41]

The representation of truth passed on from the Athens of Marathon to the philosophers. When Aristophanes complained that the tragedy died from philosophy, he had at least an inkling of what actually took place, that is, of the *translatio* of truth from the people of Athens to Socrates. The tragedy died because the citizens of Athens no longer were representable by the suffering heroes. And the *drama*, the action in the Aeschylean sense, found now its hero in the new representative of truth, in its Suffering Servant Socrates—if we may use the symbol of Deutero-Isaiah. The tragedy as a literary genus was followed by the Socratic dialogue. Nor was the new theoretical truth ineffective in the social sense. Athens,

41. On the political implications of the *Troades* see Alfred Weber, *Das Tragische und die Geschichte* (Hamburg, 1943), pp. 385 ff.

to be sure, could be no longer its representative; but Plato and Aristotle themselves created the new type of society that could become the carrier of their truth, that is, the philosophical schools. The schools outlived the political catastrophe of the polis and became formative influences of the first order, not in Hellenistic and Roman society only, but through the ages in Islamic and Western civilizations. Again, the illusion of an impasse is created only by the fascination with the fate of Athens.

9

The result of the inquiry can now be summarized. To the existential meaning of representation must be added the sense in which society is the representative of a transcendent truth. The two meanings refer to aspects of one problem in so far as, first, the existential representative of a society is its active leader in the representation of truth; and in so far as, second, a government by consent of the citizen-body presupposes the articulation of the individual citizens to the point where they can be made active participants in the representation of truth through Peitho, through persuasion. The precise nature of this many-sided problem, furthermore, came historically into the range of reflective consciousness through the discovery of the psyche as the sensorium of transcendence. The discoverer, the mystic philosopher, became as a consequence the representative of the new truth; and the symbols in which he explicated his experience formed the nucleus of a theory of social order. And, finally, it was possible to penetrate the mystery of critical clarification. Genetically it proved to consist in the discovery of the psyche and of its anthropological and theological truth, while critically it consisted in the measuring of the symbols in reality by the standards of the new truth.

III

THE STRUGGLE FOR REPRESENTATION IN THE ROMAN EMPIRE

☼

1

THE preceding lecture has shown that the problems of representation were not exhausted by internal articulation of a society in historical existence. Society as a whole proved to represent a transcendent truth; and, hence, the concept of representation in the existential sense had to be supplemented by a concept of transcendental representation. And on this new level of the problem, then, arose a further complication through the development of theory as a truth about man in rivalry with the truth represented by society. Even this complication, however, is not the last one. The field of competitive types of truth is historically broadened by the appearance of Christianity. All three of these types enter into the great struggle for the monopoly of existential representation in the Roman Empire. This struggle will form the subject matter of the present lecture; but, before approaching the subject itself, a few terminological and general theoretical points must be clarified. This procedure of bracketing out the general issues will avoid awkward digressions and explanations which otherwise would have to interrupt the political study proper when the questions become acute.

Terminologically, it will be necessary to distinguish between three types of truth. The first of these types is the truth represented by the early empires; it shall be designated as "cosmological truth." The second type of truth appears in the

political culture of Athens and specifically in tragedy; it shall
be called "anthropological truth"—with the understanding
that the term covers the whole range of problems connected
with the psyche as the sensorium of transcendence. The third
type of truth that appears with Christianity shall be called
"soteriological truth."

The terminological differentiation between the second and
third types is theoretically necessary because the Platonic-
Aristotelian complex of experiences was enlarged by Christianity in a decisive point. This point of difference can be established perhaps best by reflecting for a moment on the
Aristotelian conception of *philia politike*, of political friendship.[1] Such friendship is for Aristotle the substance of political society; it consists in *homonoia*, in spiritual agreement
between men; and it is possible between men only in so far as
these men live in agreement with the nous, that is, the divin-
est part in themselves. All men participate in the nous, though
in varying degrees of intenseness; and, hence, the love of men
for their own noetic self will make the nous the common bond
between them.[2] Only in so far as men are equal through the
love of their noetic self is friendship possible; the social bond
between unequals will be weak. On this occasion, now, Aristotle formulated his thesis that friendship was impossible between God and man because of their radical inequality.[3]

The impossibility of *philia* between God and man may be
considered typical for the whole range of anthropological
truth. The experiences that were explicated into a theory of
man by the mystic philosophers had in common the accent on
the human side of the orientation of the soul toward divinity.
The soul orients itself toward a God who rests in his immov-
able transcendence; it reaches out toward divine reality, but it

1. Aristotle *Nicomachean Ethics* 1167b3–4.
2. *Ibid.* 1166a1 ff.; 1167a22 ff.; 1177a12–18; 1177b27—1178a8.
3. *Ibid.* 1158b29—1159a13.

does not meet an answering movement from beyond. The Christian bending of God in grace toward the soul does not come within the range of these experiences—though, to be sure, in reading Plato one has the feeling of moving continuously on the verge of a breakthrough into this new dimension. The experience of mutuality in the relation with God, of the *amicitia* in the Thomistic sense, of the grace which imposes a supernatural form on the nature of man, is the specific difference of Christian truth.[4] The revelation of this grace in history, through the incarnation of the Logos in Christ, intelligibly fulfilled the adventitious movement of the spirit in the mystic philosophers. The critical authority over the older truth of society which the soul had gained through its opening and its orientation toward the unseen measure was now confirmed through the revelation of the measure itself. In this sense, then, it may be said that the fact of revelation is its content.[5]

In speaking in such terms about the experiences of the mystic philosophers and their fulfilment through Christianity, an assumption concerning history is implied that must be explicated. It is the assumption that the substance of history consists in the experiences in which man gains the understanding of his humanity and together with it the understanding of its limits. Philosophy and Christianity have endowed man with the stature that enables him, with historical effectiveness, to play the role of rational contemplator and pragmatic master of a nature which has lost its demonic terrors. With equal historical effectiveness, however, limits were placed on human grandeur; for Christianity has concentrated demonism into the permanent danger of a fall from the spirit—that is man's only

4. Thomas Aquinas *Contra Gentiles* iii. 91.

5. This conception of revelation as well as of its function in a philosophy of history is more fully elaborated in H. Richard Niebuhr, *The Meaning of Revelation* (New York, 1946), esp. pp. 93, 109 ff.

by the grace of God—into the autonomy of his own self, from the *amor Dei* into the *amor sui*. The insight that man in his mere humanity, without the *fides caritate formata*, is demonic nothingness has been brought by Christianity to the ultimate border of clarity which by tradition is called revelation.

This assumption about the substance of history, now, entails consequences for a theory of human existence in society which, under the pressure of a secularized civilization, even philosophers of rank sometimes hesitate to accept without reservation. You have seen, for instance, that Karl Jaspers considered the age of the mystic philosophers the axis time of mankind, in preference to the Christian epoch, disregarding the ultimate clarity concerning the *conditio humana* that was brought by Christianity. And Henri Bergson had hesitations on the same issue—though in his last conversations, published posthumously by Sertillanges, he seemed inclined to accept the consequence of his own philosophy of history.[6] This consequence can be formulated as the principle that a theory of human existence in society must operate within the medium of experiences which have differentiated historically. There is a strict correlation between the theory of human existence and the historical differentiation of experiences in which this existence has gained its self-understanding. Neither is the theorist permitted to disregard any part of this experience for one reason or another; nor can he take his position at an Archimedean point outside the substance of history. Theory is bound by history in the sense of the differentiating experiences. Since the maximum of differentiation was achieved through Greek philosophy and Christianity, this means concretely that theory is bound to move within the historical horizon of classic and Christian experiences. To recede from the maximum of differentiation is theoretical retrogression; it will result in the various types of derailment which Plato has characterized as

6. A. D. Sertillanges, *Avec Henri Bergson* (Paris, 1941).

doxa.[7] Whenever in modern intellectual history a revolt against the maximum of differentiation was undertaken systematically, the result was the fall into anti-Christian nihilism, into the idea of the superman in one or the other of its variants—be it the progressive superman of Condorcet, the positivistic superman of Comte, the materialistic superman of Marx, or the Dionysiac superman of Nietzsche. This problem of the antitheoretical derailments, however, will be dealt with in greater detail in the second part of these lectures, in the study of modern political mass movements. The principle of correlation between theory and the maximal experiential differentiation that will govern the following analysis should have become sufficiently clear for the present purpose.

2

The analysis will again be conducted in accordance with the Aristotelian procedure. It will start from the self-interpretation of society—with the understanding, however, that self-interpretation now includes the interpretations by theorists and saints.

The various types of truth, the Platonic *typoi peri theologias*, which entered into competition became the subject of formal

7. The dependence of a progress of theorizing on the differentiating experiences of transcendence has become a major problem in intellectual history. Theoretical superiority as a factor in the victory of Christianity over paganism in the Roman Empire, for instance, is strongly stressed in Charles N. Cochrane, *Christianity and Classical Culture: A Study of Thought and Action from Augustus to Augustine* (New York, 1944), esp. chaps. xi and xii. The technical superiority of Christian over Greek metaphysics has, furthermore, received careful treatment in Étienne Gilson, *L'Esprit de la philosophie médiévale* (2d ed.; Paris, 1948), esp. chaps. iii, iv, and v. The continuity of development from Greek into Christian theoretical explication of experiences of transcendence, on the other hand, was clarified by Werner Jaeger's *Theology of the Early Greek Philosophers* (Oxford, 1947). In this contemporary debate comes to life again the great problem of the *praeparatio evangelica* that had been understood by Clement of Alexandria when he referred to Hebrew Scripture and Greek philosophy as the two Old Testaments of Christianity (*Stromates* vi). On this question see also Serge Boulgakof, *Le Paraclet* (Paris, 1946), pp. 10 ff.

classification. The earliest extant classification precedes the Christian Era; it was made by Varro in his *Antiquities*, a work that was completed about 47 B.c. A reclassification was undertaken toward the end of the Roman period by St. Augustine in his *Civitas Dei*. The two works are related to each other in so far as the Varronic classification is preserved through the account and criticism of St. Augustine.[8]

According to the Augustinian account, Varro distinguished three kinds (*genera*) of theology—the mythical, the physical, and the civil.[9] The mythical is the theology of the poets, the physical of the philosophers, the civil of the peoples[10] or, in another version, of the *principes civitatis*.[11] The Greek terminology as well as the formulation in detail indicates that Varro had not invented the classification but had taken it from a Greek, probably a Stoic source.

St. Augustine in his turn adopted the Varronic types with certain modifications. In the first place, he translated the mythical and physical theologies into his Latin as fabulous and natural, thereby giving currency to the term "natural theology," which has remained in use to this day.[12] Second, he treated the fabulous as part of civil theology because of the cult character of dramatic poetry about the gods.[13] As a consequence, the Varronic kinds would be reduced to civil and natural theologies. The reduction is not without interest, because quite probably it is due, through various intermediaries, to the influence of a saying of Antisthenes that "according to *nomos* there are many gods, while according to *physis* there is

8. A partial reconstruction of Varro's work on the basis of the Augustinian account is to be found in R. Agahd, *De Varronis rerum divinarum libris I, XIV, XV, XVI* (Leipzig, 1896).

9. Augustinus *Civitas Dei* (ed. Dombart) vi. 5.

10. *Ibid*. 5.   11. *Ibid*. iv. 27.

12. *Ibid*. vi. 5. On Augustine's use of the term "natural theology" see Werner Jaeger, *The Theology of the Early Greek Philosophers* (Oxford, 1947), pp. 2ff.

13. *Op. cit*. vi. 6.

one." In opposition to *physis*, *nomos* would embrace culture both poetic and political as the work of man—an accentuation of the human origin of pagan gods which must have appealed to St. Augustine.[14] And since, finally, Christianity and its supernatural truth had to be included in the kinds of theology, the result was again a tripartite division of the types into civil, natural, and supernatural theologies.

3

The classifications arose incidental to the struggle for representation; they were loaded with the tensions of self-consciousness and opposition. The analysis of these tensions may profitably be opened by reflecting on an oddity of the *Civitas Dei*. The book, as far as its political function is concerned, was a *livre de circonstance*. The conquest of Rome by Alaric in A.D. 410 had aroused the pagan population of the Empire; the fall of Rome was considered a punishment by the gods for the neglect of their cult. The dangerous wave of resentment seemed to require a comprehensive critique and refutation of pagan theology in general and of the arguments against Christianity in particular. The Augustinian solution of the task was curious, because it assumed the form of a critical attack on Varro's *Antiquities*, a work that had been written almost five hundred years earlier for the purpose of bolstering the waning enthusiasm of the Romans for their civil religion. The enthusiasm had not markedly increased since Varro; and the non-Roman population could hardly be suspected of more zeal than the Romans themselves. At the time of St. Augustine the vast majority of pagans in the Empire were, in fact, adherents of the mysteries of Eleusis, of Isis, of Attis, and of Mithra rather

14. See on this question Jaeger, *op. cit.*, p. 3, nn. 8–10. The classification of Antisthenes, together with its quotations in Minucius Felix, Lactantius, and Clement of Alexandria, is to be found in Eduard Zeller, *Die Philosophie der Griechen*, II/1 (5th ed.; Leipzig, 1922), 329, n.1.

than of the cult divinities of republican Rome; and, nevertheless, he barely mentioned the mysteries while he submitted the
civil theology to the detailed criticism of Books vi–vii.

The answer to the puzzle cannot be found in a statistics of
religious affiliation; it must rather be sought in the issue of
public representation of transcendent truth. The loyalists of
the Roman civil religion were, indeed, a comparatively small
group, but the Roman cult had remained the state cult of the
Empire well into the second half of the fourth century.
Neither Constantine nor his Christian successors had considered it advisable to abandon their function as the *pontifex
maximus* of Rome. Serious inroads were made, to be sure, into
the freedom of the pagan cults under the sons of Constantine,
but the great blow came only under Theodosius with the
famous law of 380 which made orthodox Christianity the
obligatory creed for all subjects of the Empire, branded all dis-
sidents as foolish and demented, and threatened them with the
eternal wrath of God as well as with the punishment of the
emperor.[15] Up to this date the enforcement of imperial legislation in religious matters had been rather spotty, as might well
be expected in the predominantly pagan environment; and,
judging by the number of repetitious laws, it cannot have been
overeffective even after 380. Anyway, in the city of Rome the
laws were simply set aside, and the official cult had remained
pagan. Now, however, the attack was seriously concentrated
on this sensitive center. In 382 Gratianus, the emperor of the
West, abandoned his title of *pontifex maximus*, rejecting thereby the responsibility of the government for the sacrifices of
Rome; at the same time, furthermore, the cult endowment was
abolished, so that the expensive sacrifices and festivals could
no longer be continued; and, most decisively, the image and
the Altar of Victoria were removed from the assembly room of

15. *Codex Theodosianus* xvi. i. 2.

the Senate. The gods of Rome were no longer represented even in the capital of the Empire.[16]

Most gratifyingly—from the pagan point of view—Gratianus was murdered in 383, the city was threatened by the anti-emperor Maximus, and a poor harvest was causing a famine. The gods obviously showed their anger, and the time seemed propitious to request rescinding of the measures, and in particular restoration of the Altar of Victoria, from the young Valentinian II. The petition of the Pagan party in the Senate was handed to the emperor in 384 by Symmachus; regrettably, though, the harvest of 384 was excellent and thus furnished a cheap argument to St. Ambrose, who defended the Christian side.[17]

The memorandum of Symmachus was a noble plea for the Roman tradition, based on the ancient principle of *do-ut-des*. Neglect of the cult will lead to disaster; Victoria especially has benefited the Empire and should not be despised;[18] and then, with a touch of tolerance, the author pleads that everybody should be permitted to venerate the one divinity in his own way.[19] St. Ambrose in his answer could easily dispose, as we have hinted, of the *do-ut-des* principle;[20] and it was not difficult to show that the noble tolerance of Symmachus was less impressive if one considered that in practice it implied compulsion for Christian senators to participate in the sacrifices for Victoria.[21] The decisive argument, however, was contained in the sentence which formulated the principle of representation: "While all men who are subject to Roman rule serve

16. On the affair of the Altar of Victoria see Hendrik Berkhof, *Kirche und Kaiser: Eine Untersuchung der Entstehung der byzantinischen und der theokratischen Staatsauffassung im vierten Jahrhundert*, trans. Gottfried W. Locher (Zollikon-Zurich, 1947), pp. 174 ff.; Gaston Boissier, *La Fin du paganisme*, Vol. II (2d ed.; Paris, 1894).

17. Ambrosius *Epistolae* xvii and xviii. The *Relatio Symmachi urbis praefecti* is appended to Ambrosius' Letter XVII (Migne, Pl. XVI).

18. *Relatio Symmachi* 3-4.   20. Ambrosius *Epistolae* xviii. 4 ff.

19. *Ibid.* 6 and 10.   21. *Ibid.* xvii. 9.

(*militare*) you emperors and princes of the earth, you your-
selves serve (*militare*) the omnipotent God and holy faith.''[22]
It almost sounds like the Mongol Order of God that was discussed in the preceding lecture, but, in fact, it is its inversion.
The formulation of St. Ambrose does not justify the imperial
monarchy by pointing to the monarchical rule of God—
though this problem also became acute in the Roman Empire,
as will be seen a bit later on. It does not speak of any rule at
all but of service. The subjects serve the prince on earth as
their existential representative, and St. Ambrose had no illusions about the source of the imperial position: the legions
make Victoria, he remarked contemptuously, not Victoria the
Empire.[23] Political society in historical existence begins to
show the hue of temporality as distinguished from spiritual
order. Above this temporal sphere of service on the part of the
subjects, then, rises the emperor, who serves only God. The
appeal of St. Ambrose does not go to the imperial ruler but to
the Christian who happens to be the incumbent of the office.
The Christian ruler is admonished not to pretend ignorance
and let things drift; if he does not show his zeal in the faith
positively as he should, he must at least not give his assent to
idolatry and pagan cults.[24] A Christian emperor knows that he
should honor only the altar of Christ, and ''the voice of our
Emperor be the echo of Christ.''[25] In barely veiled language
the bishop threatens the emperor with excommunication if he
should grant the petition of the Senate.[26] The truth of Christ
cannot be represented by the *imperium mundi* but only by the
service of God.

These are the beginnings of a theocratic conception of rulership in the strict sense, theocracy not meaning a rule by the
priesthood but the recognition by the ruler of the truth of

22. *Ibid.* 1.
23. *Ibid.* xviii. 30.   25. *Ibid.* xviii. 10.
24. *Ibid.* xvii. 2.   26. *Ibid.* xvii. 14.

God.[27] The conception unfolded fully in the next generation in the Augustinian image of the *imperator felix* in *Civitas Dei* v. 24–26. The happiness of the emperor cannot be measured by the external successes of his rule; St. Augustine makes a special point of the successes of pagan and the misfortunes and murderous ends of some Christian rulers; the true happiness of the emperor can be measured only by his conduct as a Christian on the throne. The chapters on the *imperator felix* are the first "Mirror of the Prince"; they stand at the beginning of the medieval literary genus and have immeasurably influenced the idea and practice of Western rulership ever since Charlemagne made them his guidebook.

In the affair of the Altar of Victoria, St. Ambrose won. In the following years the situation tightened still further. In 391 a law of Theodosius prohibited all pagan ceremonies in the city of Rome;[28] a law of his sons, in 396, removed the last immunities of pagan priests and hierophants;[29] a law of 407 for Italy suppressed all allocations for *epula sacra* and ritual games, ordered the removal of statues from the temples, the destruction of altars, and the return of the temples *ad usum publicum*.[30] When in 410 Rome fell to the Gothic invaders, the cult of Rome was indeed a living issue for the victims of the recent antipagan legislation; and the fall of the city could well be propagandized as the revenge of the gods for the specific insults to the civil religion of Rome.

4

The curiosity has been cleared up only to give way to another one. The Christian protagonists in this struggle were not concerned with the salvation of pagan souls; they were

27. On the struggle for theocracy in this sense see Berkhof, *op. cit.*, chap. viii: "Um die Theokratie."

28. *Codex Theodosianus* xvi. x. 10.

29. *Ibid.* x. 14.   30. *Ibid.* 19.

engaged in a political struggle about the public cult of the Empire. To be sure, the appeal of St. Ambrose went to the Christian on the throne; and about the sincerity of his intentions there can be no doubt when we remember his clash with Theodosius in 390, on occasion of the massacre of Thessalonica. Nevertheless, when the Christian is an emperor, his Christian conduct will put the pagans into the same position in which the Christians were under pagan emperors. It is curious that both St. Ambrose and St. Augustine, while bitterly engaged in the struggle for existential representation of Christianity, should have been almost completely blind to the nature of the issue. Nothing seemed to be at stake but the truth of Christianity versus the untruth of paganism. This does not mean that they were quite unaware of the existential issue involved; on the contrary, the *Civitas Dei* has its peculiar fascination because St. Augustine, while obviously not understanding the existential problem of paganism, was rather worried that something eluded him. His attitude toward Varro's civil theology resembled that of an enlightened intellectual toward Christianity—he simply could not understand that an intelligent person would seriously maintain such nonsense. He escaped from his difficulty by assuming that Varro, the Stoic philosopher, could not have believed in the Roman divinities but that, under cover of a respectful account, he wanted to expose them to ridicule.[31] It will be necessary to hear Varro himself, as well as his friend Cicero, in order to find the point which eluded St. Augustine.

The elusive point was reported by St. Augustine himself with great care; it obviously disconcerted him. Varro, in his *Antiquities*, had treated first of "human things" and then only of the "divine things" of Rome.[32] First, the city must exist; then it can proceed to institute its cults. "As the painter is

31. Augustinus *Civitas Dei* vi. 2.
32. *Ibid.* 3.

prior to the painting, and the architect prior to the building, so are the cities prior to the institutions of the cities."[33] This Varronic conception that the gods were instituted by political society aroused the incomprehending irritation of St. Augustine. On the contrary, he insisted, "true religion is not instituted by some terrestrial city," but the true God, the inspirator of true religion, "has instituted the celestial city."[34] Varro's attitude seemed particularly reprehensible because the things human to which he gave priority were not even universally human but just Roman.[35] Moreover, St. Augustine suspected him of deception because Varro admitted that he would have put the things divine first if he had intended to treat of the nature of the gods exhaustively;[36] and because he, furthermore, suggested that in matters of religion much is true that the people ought not to know and much false that the people ought not to suspect.[37]

What St. Augustine could not understand was the compactness of Roman experience, the inseparable community of gods and men in the historically concrete *civitas*, the simultaneousness of human and divine institution of a social order. For him the order of human existence had already separated into the *civitas terrena* of profane history and the *civitas coelestis* of divine institution. Nor was the understanding facilitated by the apparently somewhat primitive formulations of the encyclopedist Varro. The more supple Cicero voiced the same convictions as his friend with more conceptual refinement through the figures of his *De natura deorum*, especially through the *princeps civis* and *pontifex* Cotta. In the debate about the existence of the gods there stand against each other the opinions of the philosopher and of the Roman social leader. Subtly Cicero suggests the different sources of authority when he opposes

33. *Ibid.* 4.
34. *Ibid.*   36. *Ibid.* iv. 31; vi. 4.
35. *Ibid.*   37. *Ibid.* iv. 31.

the *princeps philosophiae* Socrates[38] to the *princeps civis* Cotta;[39] the *auctoritas philosophi* clashes with the *auctoritas majorum*.[40] The dignitary of the Roman cult is not inclined to doubt the immortal gods and their worship whatever anybody may say. In matters of religion he will follow the pontiffs who preceded him in the office and no Greek philosophers. The auspices of Romulus and the rites of Numa laid the foundations of the state which never could have achieved its greatness without the ritual conciliation of the immortals in its favor.[41] He accepts the gods on the authority of the forebears, but he is willing to listen to the opinion of others; and not without irony he invites Balbus to give the reasons, *rationem*, for his religious beliefs which as a philosopher he ought to have, while he the pontiff is compelled to believe the forebears without reason.[42]

The Varronic and Ciceronian expositions are precious documents for the theorist. The Roman thinkers live firmly in their political myth but at the same time have been made aware of the fact through contact with Greek philosophy; the contact has not affected the solidity of their sentiments but only equipped them with the means of elucidating their position. The conventional treatment of Cicero is apt to overlook that in his work something considerably more interesting is to be found than a variant of Stoicism—something that no Greek source can give us, that is, the archaic experience of social order before its dissolution through the experience of the mystic philosophers. In the Greek sources this archaic stratum never can really be touched, because the earliest literary documents, the poems of Homer and Hesiod, are already magnificently free reorganizations of mythical material—in the case of Hesiod even with the conscious opposition of a truth found

---

38. Cicero *De natura deorum* ii. 167.

39. *Ibid*. 168.   41. *Ibid*.

40. *Ibid*. iii. 5.   42. *Ibid*. 6.

by him as an individual to the lie, the *pseudos*, of the older myth. It was perhaps the unsettlement in the wake of the Doric invasion that broke the compactness of Greek social existence so much earlier, a type of shock that never disturbed Rome. Anyway, Rome was an archaic survival in the Hellenistic civilization of the Mediterranean and still more so with its advancing Christianization; one might compare the situation with the role of Japan in a civilizational environment that is dominated by Western ideas.

Romans like Cicero understood the problem quite well. In his *De re publica*, for instance, he deliberately opposed the Roman style of dealing with matters of political order to the Greek style. In the debate about the best political order (*status civitatis*), again a *princeps civis*, Scipio, takes his stand against Socrates. Scipio refuses to discuss the best order in the manner of the Platonic Socrates; he will not build up a "fictitious" order before his audience but will rather give an account of the origins of Rome.[43] The order of Rome is superior to any other —this dogma is heavily put down as the condition of debate.[44] The discussion itself may freely range through all topics of Greek learning, but this learning will have meaning only in so far as it can be brought usefully to bear on problems of Roman order. The highest rank, to be sure, is held by the man who can add the "foreign learning" to his ancestral customs; but, if a choice must be made between the two ways of life, the *vita civilis* of the statesman is preferable to the *vita quieta* of the sage.[45]

The thinker who can speak of philosophy as a "foreign learning," to be respected but nevertheless to be considered as a spice that will add perfection to superiority, has, one may safely say, understood neither the nature of the spiritual revolution that found its expression in philosophy nor the nature

43. Cicero *De re publica* ii. 3.
44. *Ibid.* i. 70; ii. 2.   45. *Ibid.* iii. 5–6.

of its universal claim upon man. The peculiar way in which Cicero mixes his respect for Greek philosophy with amused contempt indicates that the truth of theory, while sensed as an enlargement of the intellectual and moral horizon, could have no existential meaning for a Roman. Rome was the Rome of its gods into every detail of daily routine; to participate experientially in the spiritual revolution of philosophy would have implied the recognition that the Rome of the ancestors was finished and that a new order was in the making into which the Romans would have to merge—as the Greeks had to merge, whether they liked it or not, into the imperial constructions of Alexander and the Diadochi and finally of Rome. The Rome of the generation of Cicero and Caesar was simply not so far gone as was the Athens of the fourth century B.C. which engendered Plato and Aristotle. The Roman substance preserved its strength well into the Empire, and it really petered out only in the troubles of the third century A.D. Only then had come the time for Rome to merge into the empire of its own making; and only then did the struggle among the various types of alternative truth, among philosophies, oriental cults, and Christianity, enter into the crucial phase where the existential representative, the emperor, had to decide which transcendental truth he would represent now that the myth of Rome had lost its ordering force. For a Cicero such problems did not exist, and when he encountered them in his "foreign learning" he emasculated the inexorable threat: the Stoic idea that every man had two countries, the polis of his birth and the cosmopolis, he transformed deftly into the idea that every man had indeed two fatherlands, the countryside of his birth, for Cicero his Arpinum, and Rome.[46] The cosmopolis of the philosophers was realized in historical existence; it was the *imperium Romanum*.[47]

46. Cicero *De legibus* ii. 5.

47. A tendency toward this identification is discernible before Cicero, especially in Polybius (see Harry A. Wolfson, *Philo* [Cambridge, Mass., 1947], II, 419 ff.).

5

The strength of its archaic compactness secured for Rome the survival in the struggle for empire. This successful survival, however, raises one of the great questions of history, that is, the question how the institutions of republican Rome —which in themselves were no more fit for the organization of an empire than the institutions of Athens or any other Greek polis—could be adapted in such a manner that an emperor would emerge from them as the existential representative of the Mediterranean *orbis terrarum*. The process of transformation is obscure in many details and will remain so forever because of the scarcity of sources. Nevertheless, the careful analysis and evaluation of the scanty materials by two generations of scholars has resulted in a coherent picture of the process, as it can be found in the penetrating study of the principate by Anton von Premerstein.[48]

The main burden of adaptation to imperial rule was not carried by the republican constitution at all. To be sure, the number of senators could be increased by appointment of provincials in order to make it more representative of the Empire, as it had been done already by Caesar; and citizenship could be extended to Italy and successively to other provinces. But a development of representation through elections on a popular basis from the provinces of the Empire was impossible in face of the constitutional inflexibility which Rome shared with the other poleis. The adaptation had to rely on social institutions outside the constitution proper; and the main institution, which developed into the imperial office, was that of the *princeps civis* or *princeps civitatis*, of the social and political leader.

In earlier republican history the term "princeps" designated

48. Anton von Premerstein, *Vom Werden und Wesen des Prinzipats*, ed. Hans Volkmann ("Abhandlungen der Bayerischen Akademie der Wissenschaften, Phil.-hist. Abt., Neue Folge," Heft 15 [Munich, 1937]).

any leading citizen. At the core of the institution was the patronate, a relationship created through the fact of various favors—political aid, loans, personal gifts, etc.—between a man of social influence and a man of lesser social rank in need of such favors. Through tendering and accepting such favors a sacred bond under the sanction of the gods was created between the two men; the accepting man, the client, became the follower of the patron, and their relationship was governed by *fides*, by loyalty. In the nature of the case, the patron had to be a man of social rank and wealth. The formation of a considerable clientele would be the privilege of members of the patricio-plebeian nobility; and the most important senators of consular rank would at the same time be the most powerful patrons. Such patrons of highest official rank were the *principes civitatis;* and of their number one could be a leader of unquestioned superiority if he belonged to one of the old patrician families and held the position of a *princeps senatus* and perhaps, in addition, that of the *pontifex maximus*. Roman society, thus, was a complicated network of personal followerships—hierarchically organized in so far as the clients of a powerful patron might themselves be patrons of a numerous clientele, and competitively organized in so far as the principes were rivals in the struggle for high offices and for political power in general.[49] The substance of Roman politics in the late republican period was the struggle for power among wealthy leaders of personal parties, based on the patrocinial relationship. Among such leaders, then, agreements were possible, the so-called *amicitiae;* and the breach of agreement led to formal feuds, the *inimicitiae*, preceded by mutual accusations, the *altercatio*, which in the period of the civil wars assumed the form of propaganda pamphlets to the public detailing the infamous conduct of the opponent. Such *inimicitiae* were distinguished from formal wars, from a *bellum justum* of

49. *Ibid.*, pp. 15–16.

the Roman people against a public enemy. The last war of Octavianus against Antony and Cleopatra, for instance, was juridically conducted with great care as a formal war against Cleopatra and as an *inimicitia* against Antony and his Roman clientele.[50]

The transformation of the original principate into a few giant party organizations was caused by the military expansion of Rome and the ensuing social changes. The wars of the third century, with their conquests in Greece, Africa, and Spain, had raised an insolvable problem of logistics. The overseas territories could not be conquered and held by armies that were to be renewed by annual levies; it proved impossible to transport the old contingents home every year and to replace them by new ones. The provincial armies of necessity had to become professional, with ten and twenty years of service. The returning veterans were a homeless mass that had to be taken care of by land allotments, by colonization, or by permission to reside within the city of Rome with the attendant privileges. For obtaining such benefits the veterans had to rely on their military commanders who were principes, with the result that whole armies became part of the clientele of a princeps. If anything is significant for the evolution of late republican Rome, it is the fact that the class discipline of the nobility held out for a whole century before the powerful new party leaders turned against the Senate and transformed the political life of Rome into a private contest among themselves. Moreover, with the enormous enlargement of the clienteles, and their increase by armed forces for warfare and street fights, it became necessary to formalize the previously formless relationships through special oaths by which the client was bound in *fides* to his patron. On this point the sources are particularly scanty, but it is possible nevertheless to trace such oaths in increasing numbers and varieties after 100 B.C.[51] And,

50. *Ibid.*, p. 37.   51. *Ibid.*, pp. 26 ff.

finally, the structure of the system was determined by the hereditary character of the clientele. The inheritance of the clientele was a factor of considerable importance in the course of the civil wars of the first century B.C. In his early struggle with Antony, for instance, Octavianus had the great asset of Caesar's veteran colonies in Campania which had become his clientele as Caesar's heir.[52] And the settlement of inherited soldier clienteles even determined the theater of war. The Pompeians, for instance, had to be fought down in Spain because the Magnus had colonized his soldiers in the Iberian Peninsula.[53]

The emergence of the principate, thus, may be described as an evolution of the patronate—which for the rest continued to exist in its modest form well into the imperial period. When the patron was a *princeps civis*, the clientele would become an instrument of political power, and with the inclusion of veteran armies it would become an instrument of military power in rivalry with the constitutional armed forces. Political influence, wealth, and military clientele determined and increased one another mutually in so far as the political position secured the military command, necessary for the conquest of provinces and their profitable exploitation, while the exploitation of the provinces was necessary for supporting the clientele with spoils and land, and the clientele was necessary to hold political influence. With the reduction of the competitors to a few great party leaders the breaking point of constitutional legality was reached, especially when the Senate and the magistrates themselves were divided between the clienteles of the protagonists. In the life of each of the great party leaders of the first century there came the time when he had to decide upon his transgression of the line between legality and illegality—the most famous of these decisions being Caesar's crossing of the Rubicon.[54] And Octavianus, a cool and

---

52. *Ibid.*, p. 24.   53. *Ibid.*, pp. 16 ff.   54. *Ibid.*, pp. 24 ff.

calculating politician, chose to conduct his last war with Antony as an *inimicitia* because a declaration of Antony as public enemy could have provoked the same declaration against himself, since both consuls and part of the Senate were in Antony's camp. The mutual declaration as public enemies would have split Rome, as it were, into two hostile states fighting each other; and the shaking of the Republic to its constitutional foundations might have had the same disastrous results as the parallel situation in the death struggle between Caesar and Pompey—with the murder of the victorious leader in the year after his triumph at the hands of republican sentimentalists. The principate, thus, evolved through the reduction of the great patrocinial principes to the three of the triumvirates, then to Antony and Octavianus, and finally to the monopolization of the position by the victor of Actium.[55]

The representative order of Rome after Actium was a skilful combination of the old republican constitution with the new existential representation of the empire people by the princeps. The direct relationship between the princeps and the people was secured through the extension of the clientele oath to the people at large. In 32 B.C. Octavianus, before entering on his struggle with Antony, had exacted such an oath from Italy and the western provinces, the so-called conjuration of the West; it was an oath of loyalty rendered to Octavianus *pro partibus suis*, that is, to him as the leader of a party.[56] Concerning the extension of the oath to the eastern provinces, which must have taken place after Actium, no sources are available.[57] Nevertheless, the oath to the princeps in the form of 32 B.C. became a permanent institution. It was sworn again to the successors of Augustus on occasion of their ascent to power,[58] and beginning with Caius Caligula it was renewed

55. *Ibid.*, p. 37.
56. *Ibid.*, pp. 42 ff.
57. *Ibid.*, p. 52.   58. *Ibid.*, pp. 56 ff.

annually.[59] The patrocinial articulation of a group into leader and followers had expanded into the form of imperial representation.

6

The patrocinial, expanded into the imperial, principate was the institution that made the new ruler the existential representative for the vast agglomeration of conquered territories and peoples. Obviously, the instrument was brittle. Its effectiveness depended on the experience of the patrocinial relation as a sacramental bond in the Roman sense. The new Augustus saw the problem; and his legislation for moral and religious reform must be understood, at least in part, as the attempt of reinforcing sacramental sentiments which had been waning even among the Romans at the time of Varro's *Antiquities*. In face of the vast oriental population the task was hopeless, especially since the Easterners streamed into Rome in ever increasing numbers and were clinging to their non-Roman cults in spite of all prohibitions; and the task became still more hopeless when the emperors themselves ceased to be Romans, when the Julian dynasty was followed by the provincial Flavians, by the Spaniards, the Syrians, and the Illyrians.

The remedy for the sacramental deficiency in the position of the emperor was found only gradually, on a tortuous path of experimentation and failure. The divinization of the emperor, following the model of Hellenistic kingship, proved insufficient. It also had to be determined which divine power he represented among the mass of cult divinities in the Empire. Under the pressure of this problem the religious culture of the Roman Mediterranean underwent a process which usually is called syncretism, or *theokrasia*, mixture of the gods. The evolution is not singular; it is in substance the same process which the Near Eastern empires had undergone at an earlier time, the

59. *Ibid.*, pp. 60 ff.

process of reinterpreting the multitude of local cult divinities in the politically unified area as the aspects of one highest god who then became the empire-god. Under the peculiar conditions of the civilizationally mixed Roman area, experimentation with such a highest god was not easy. On the one hand, the god could not be a conceptual abstraction but had to have an intelligible relationship to one or more concretely experienced gods who were known as high; on the other hand, if the relationship to a concretely existing god became too close, his value as a god above all known special gods was in danger. The attempt of Elagabalus (218–22) to introduce the Baal of Emesa as the highest god to Rome miscarried. A circumcised Caesar who married a Vestal virgin in order to symbolize the union between Baal and Tanit proved too much of a strain on the Roman tradition. He was murdered by his praetorian guards. The Illyrian Aurelian (270–75) tried with better success when he declared a sufficiently nondescript sun-god, the *Sol Invictus*, as the highest god of the Empire and himself as his descendant and representative. With some variation under Diocletian (284–305) the system lasted until A.D. 313.

The fact that the empire cult was a subject of experimentation should not deceive us, however, about the religious seriousness with which these experiments were undertaken. Spiritually the late Roman summodeism had approached closely enough to Christianity to make conversion almost a slight transition. There is extant the prayer of Licinius before his battle against Maximinus Daza in 313. An angel appeared to Licinius in the night and assured him of victory if he and the army would pray it:

> Highest God, we pray to thee,
> Holy God, we pray to thee.
> All justice we command to thee,
> Our weal we command to thee,
> Our realm we command to thee.

By thee we live, by thee we are victorious and
   successful.
Highest, Holy God, hear our prayers.
We raise our arms to thee,
Hear us, oh Holy, Highest God.

Story and prayer are reported by Lactantius,[60] with the understanding that the victory was due to a conversion similar to
Constantine's in the year before. The Christianity of Licinius
is at least doubtful in view of his anti-Christian policy in subsequent years, but the prayer, which could as well have been
prayed by his pagan opponent Maximinus, appeared as a confession of Christianity to Lactantius.

   The precise meaning of the surprising turn of events which
in 311–13 gave freedom to Christianity is still a matter of debate. It seems, however, that the recent interpretation by the
Dutch theologian Hendrik Berkhof has cleared up the mysterious affair as far as the sources allow.[61] The persistence and survival of the Christians under violent persecutions apparently
convinced the regents Galerius, Licinius, and Constantinus
that the Christian God was powerful enough to protect his
followers in adversity; that he was a reality that should be
treated with caution. The Edict of Galerius, of 311, explained
that as a consequence of the persecutions the Christians neither fulfilled their cult obligations to the official gods nor
worshiped their own God in proper form.[62] This observation
apparently motivated the sudden change of policy. If the powerful God of the Christians were not worshiped by his own
adherents, he might take his revenge and add to the troubles
of the rulers who prevented his worship. It was the good,
solid Roman *do-ut-des* principle.[63] In return for their new free-

60. *De mortibus persecutorum* xlvi.
61. *Op. cit.*, pp. 47 ff.
62. Lactantius, *op. cit.*, xxxiv: "cum . . . videremus nec diis eosdem cultum ac
religionem debitam exhibere, nec Christianorum Deum observare."
63. Berkhof, *op. cit.*, p. 48.

dom the edict ordered the Christians to pray for the emperor, the public weal, and their own.[64] This was no conversion to Christianity but rather an inclusion of the Christian God into the imperial system of divinity.[65] The Edict of Licinius, of 313, stated that the former anti-Christian policy had been revised "so that all that is of *divinitas* in the celestial habitat be propitious to us and all who are under our rule."[66] The curious term *divinitas* was reconcilable with official polytheism and the recognition of the *Summus Deus* of the empire religion, and at the same time it sounded monotheistic enough to make Christians happy. The suspense of meaning was probably intended — one feels in it the deft hand of the Constantine, who later, in the christological debate, insisted on the sublimely meaningless *homo-ousios*.

7

The problems of imperial theology, however, could not be solved by a linguistic compromise. The Christians were persecuted for a good reason; there was a revolutionary substance in Christianity that made it incompatible with paganism. The new alliance was bound to increase the social effectiveness of this revolutionary substance. What made Christianity so dangerous was its uncompromising, radical de-divinization of the world. The problem had been formulated perhaps most clearly by Celsus in his *True Discourse*, of *ca*. A.D. 180, the most competent pagan critique of Christianity. The Christians, he complained, reject polytheism with the argument that one cannot serve two masters.[67] This was for Celsus the "language of sedition

64. Lactantius, *op. cit.*, xxxiv *in fine*.

65. A similar interpretation is to be found in Joseph Vogt, *Constantin der Grosse und sein Jahrhundert* (Munich, 1949), pp. 154 ff.

66. *Ibid.* xlviii. I am following the reading "quidquid est divinitatis in sede coelesti," as does Berkhof, *op. cit.*, p. 51.

67. Origenes *Contra Celsum* vii. 68.

(*stasis*)."[68] The rule, he admitted, holds true among men; but nothing can be taken from God when we serve his divinity in the many manifestations of his kingdom. On the contrary, we honor and please the Most High when we honor many of those who belong to him,[69] while singling out one God and honoring him alone introduces factiousness into the divine kingdom.[70] That part will be taken only by men who stand aloof from human society and transfer their own isolating passions to God.[71] The Christians, thus, are factionals in religion and metaphysics, a sedition against the divinity which harmoniously animates the whole world in all its subdivisions. And since the various quarters of the earth were from the beginning allotted to various ruling spirits and superintending principalities,[72] the religious sedition is at the same time a political revolt. Who wishes to destroy the national cult wants to destroy the national cultures.[73] And since they all have found their place in the Empire, an attack on the cults by radical monotheists is an attack on the construction of the *imperium Romanum*. Not that it were not desirable, even in the opinion of Celsus, if Asiatics, Europeans and Libyans, Hellenes and barbarians, would agree in one *nomos*, but, he adds contemptuously, "anyone who thinks this possible knows nothing."[74] The answer of Origen in his *Contra Celsum* was that it not only was possible but that it surely would come to pass.[75] Celsus, one may say, discerned the implications of Christianity even more clearly than Cicero the implications of Greek philosophy. He understood the existential problem of polytheism; and he knew that the Christian de-divinization of the world spelled the end of a civilizational epoch and would radically transform the ethnic cultures of the age.

68. *Ibid.* viii. 2.

69. *Ibid.*

70. *Ibid.* 11.

71. *Ibid.* 2.

72. *Ibid.* v. 25.

73. *Ibid.* 26.

74. *Ibid.* viii. 72.

75. *Ibid.*

8

The belief that Christianity could be used for bolstering the political theology of the Empire, either alone or in combination with the pagan conception of a *Summus Deus*, was destined to experience a quick disappointment. Nevertheless, the belief could be entertained with reason because it found support from a Christian tendency of interpreting the one God of Christianity in the direction of a metaphysical monotheism.[76] To indulge in this experiment was an understandable temptation in the path of Eastern religions when they found themselves in the Hellenistic environment and began to express themselves in the language of Greek speculation. In fact, the Christian development in this direction was not original but followed the example of Philo Judaeus; and Philo had at his disposition already the preparatory peripatetic speculations of the first century b.c. In his *Metaphysics* Aristotle had formulated the principle: "The world does not have the will to be ruled badly; the rule of many is not good, one be the Lord."[77] In the peripatetic literature immediately preceding the time of Philo, of which the representative extant example is the pseudo-Aristotelian *De mundo*, this principle was elaborated into the great parallel constructions of imperial monarchy and divine world monarchy.[78] The divine monarchical ruler of the cosmos governs the world through his lesser messengers in the same manner in which the Persian great king governs his empire through the satraps in the provinces.[79] Philo adapted the

76. On metaphysical monotheism and its function in the political theology of the Roman Empire see Erik Peterson, *Der Monotheismus als politisches Problem: Ein Beitrag zur Geschichte der politischen Theologie im Imperium Romanum* (Leipzig, 1935). Our own analysis follows Peterson's closely.

77. Aristotle *Metaphysics* 1076a.

78. The *De mundo* is to be dated in the first century a.d. Whether it still falls in the lifetime of Philo does not matter for our purpose, because we are interested only in its typical contents.

79. *De mundo* 6.

construction to his Jewish monotheism with the purpose of forging a political propaganda instrument that would make Judaism attractive as a one-god cult in the Empire.[80] Apparently following a peripatetic source he made the Jewish God a "king of kings" in the Persian sense, while all other gods were relegated to the rank of subrulers.[81] He carefully preserved the position of the Jews as the chosen people, but he skilfully extricated them from their metaphysical impasse by making the service of Yahve the service of the God that rules the cosmos in the peripatetic sense.[82] He even referred to Plato's *Timaeus* in order to make him the God who establishes the order, the *taxis*, of the world in a constitutional sense.[83] The Jews in serving this God serve him representatively for mankind. And when he quoted the passage from Aristotle's *Metaphysics* with its Homeric verse, he insisted that the verse be considered valid for cosmic as for political rulership.[84]

The Philonic speculation was taken over by Christian thinkers.[85] The adaptation to the Christian situation in the Empire achieved its fullest development through Eusebius of Caesarea in the time of Constantine.[86] Eusebius, like many Christian thinkers before and after him, was attracted by the coincidence of the appearance of Christ with the pacification

80. On Philo's political intentions see Peterson, *op. cit.*, p. 27; Erwin R. Goodenough, *The Politics of Philo Judaeus* (New Haven, 1938); and the same author's *An Introduction to Philo Judaeus* (New Haven, 1940), chap. iii.

81. Philo *De specialibus legibus* i. 13. 18. 31; *De decalogo* 61.

82. Peterson, *op. cit.*, pp. 23 ff. In *De Abrahamo* 98 the Jews are described as the nation "dearest to God" and endowed with the gifts of priesthood and prophecy "on behalf of the whole race of men"; in *De spec. leg.* 167 the prayers of the Jews are representative for all mankind; in *De spec. leg.* 97 the high priest of the Jews prays and gives thanks not only for mankind but for the whole creation.

83. Philo *De fuga et inventione* 10. On the change of the Platonic meaning of *taxis* to the meaning of constitutional order see Peterson, *op. cit.*, pp. 28–29.

84. Philo *De confusione linguarum* 170.

85. On the absorption of Philo's speculation on divine monarchy into the Christian apologetic literature see Peterson, *op. cit.*, pp. 34–42.

86. On Eusebius see Peterson, *op. cit.*, pp. 71–76, and Berkhof, *op. cit.*, pp. 100–101.

of the Empire through Augustus. His elaborate historical work was motivated in part by his interest in the providential subjugation of formerly independent nations by the Romans. When the autonomous existence of the political entities in the Mediterranean area was broken by Augustus, the apostles of Christianity could roam unmolested through the whole Empire and spread the Gospel; they could hardly have carried out their mission unless the wrath of the "superstitious of the polis" had been kept in check by fear of Roman power.[87] The establishment of the *pax Romana* was, furthermore, not only of pragmatic importance for the expansion of Christianity but to Eusebius it seemed intimately connected with the mysteries of the Kingdom of God. In the pre-Roman period, he opined, neighbors did not live in real community but were engaged in continuous warfare with each other. Augustus dissolved the pluralistic polyarchy; with his monarchy peace descended on the earth, thus fulfilling the scriptural predictions of Mic. 4:4 and Ps. 71:7. In brief, the eschatological prophecies concerning the peace of the Lord were politicized by Eusebius when he referred them to a *pax Romana* which coincided historically with the manifestation of the Logos.[88] And, finally, Eusebius considered the work that had been begun by Augustus to be fulfilled by Constantine. In his *Tricennial Speech* he praised Constantine because in his imperial he had imitated the divine monarchy: the one *basileus* on earth represents the one God, the one King in Heaven, the one Nomos and Logos.[89] It is a return, indeed, to the imperial representation of cosmic truth.

Such harmony, of course, could not last; it had to break as soon as somewhat more sensitive Christians would get hold of the problem. The issue came to a head through the struggle

87. Eusebius *Demonstratio evangelica* iii. 7. 30–35.

88. *Ibid.*, vii. 2. 22; viii. 3. 13–15; Peterson, *op. cit.*, pp. 75–77.

89. Eusebius *Laus Constantini* 1–10; Peterson, *op. cit.*, p. 78; Berkhof, *op. cit.*, p. 102.

about the Christology. Celsus had railed at the Christians because they did not take their own monotheism seriously and
had a second God in Christ.[90] This was indeed the crucial
question that had to be settled in the christological debate
when it was stirred up by the heresy of Arius. The symbols
had to be found for interpreting the one God as three persons
in one; and with the full understanding of trinitarianism the
constructions of the Eusebian type would be finished. Under-
standably the emperors and court theologians were rather on
the Arian side; the trinitarian debate was seriously disturbing
the monotheistic ideology on which depended the conception
of the emperor as the representative of the one God. When the
resistance of Athanasius, supported by the Westerners, had
carried the trinitarian symbolism to victory, the speculations
on parallel monarchies in heaven and on earth could no longer
be continued. The language of a divine monarchy did not disappear, but it acquired a new meaning. Gregory of Nazianzus,
for instance, declared the Christians to be believers in the
divine monarchy, but, he continued, they do not believe in
the monarchy of a single person in the godhead, for such a
godhead would be a source of discord; Christians believe in
the triunity—and this triunity of God has no analogue in creation. The one person of an imperial monarch could not represent the triune divinity.[91] How impossible it had become to
operate with the idea of a trinitarian God in politics may be
illustrated by an incident from the reign of Constantine IV
Pogonatus (668–85): the army demanded that he instal his
two brothers as co-emperors in order to have on earth a representation of the divine trinity.[92] It sounds more like a joke

90. Origenes *Contra Celsum* viii. 12–16.

91. Peterson, *op. cit.*, pp. 96 ff.

92. Karl Krumbacher, *Geschichte der byzantinischen Litteratur* (2d ed.; Munich, 1897),
p. 954; E. W. Brooks, *The Successors of Heraclius to 717* (*CMH*, II, 13), p. 405; Berkhof,
op. cit., p. 144. The only other instance of an application of the Trinity to imperial rule,
as far as I know, is the *Versus Paschales* of Ausonius, A.D. 368 or shortly thereafter. In

than like a serious suggestion; and it was perhaps inevitable that in the course of events the second and third persons of the imperial trinity got their noses cut off.

The other brilliant idea of Eusebius, the idea of recognizing in the *pax Romana* the fulfilment of eschatological prophecies (an idea strongly reminiscent of Cicero's inclination to see the perfect order of the philosophers realized through Rome), fell to pieces under the pressure of a troubled age. Nevertheless, the commentary of St. Augustine on the prophecy of Ps. 45: 10 may serve as a specific assertion of the orthodox counterposition. The text is: "He maketh wars to cease unto the end of the earth." St. Augustine comments: "That we see not yet accomplished; hitherto we have wars. Between the nations there are the wars for domination. And there are also wars between the sects, between Jews, Pagans, Christians and heretics, and these wars even increase; one side fighting for truth, the other side for falsehood. In no way is there fulfilled the 'ceasing of the wars to the end of the earth'; but perhaps, we hope, it will be fulfilled."[93]

This is the end of political theology in orthodox Christianity. The spiritual destiny of man in the Christian sense cannot be represented on earth by the power organization of a political society; it can be represented only by the church. The sphere of power is radically de-divinized; it has become temporal. The double representation of man in society through church and empire lasted through the Middle Ages. The specifically modern problems of representation are connected with the re-divinization of society. The subsequent three lectures will deal with these problems.

---

this Easter poem the Trinity is seen figured on earth by Valentinian I and his co-emperors Valens and Gratianus (*Ausonius* ["Loeb Classical Library"], I, 34 ff.).

93. Augustinus *Enarratio in Psalmos* xlv. 13.

IV

GNOSTICISM—THE NATURE OF MODERNITY

☼

1

THE clash between the various types of truth in the Roman Empire ended with the victory of Christianity. The fateful result of this victory was the de-divinization of the temporal sphere of power; and it was anticipated that the specifically modern problems of representation would have something to do with a re-divinization of man and society. Both of these terms are in need of further definition, especially since the concept of modernity and with it the periodization of history depend on the meaning of re-divinization. Hence, by de-divinization shall be meant the historical process in which the culture of polytheism died from experiential atrophy, and human existence in society became reordered through the experience of man's destination, by the grace of the world-transcendent God, toward eternal life in beatific vision. By re-divinization, however, shall not be meant a revival of polytheistic culture in the Greco-Roman sense. The characterization of modern political mass movements as neopagan, which has a certain vogue, is misleading because it sacrifices the historically unique nature of modern movements to a superficial resemblance. Modern re-divinization has its origins rather in Christianity itself, deriving from components that were suppressed as heretical by the universal church. The nature of this inner-Christian tension, therefore, will have to be determined more closely.

The tension was given with the historical origin of Christianity as a Jewish messianic movement. The life of the early

Christian communities was experientially not fixed but oscillated between the eschatological expectation of the Parousia that would bring the Kingdom of God and the understanding of the church as the apocalypse of Christ in history. Since the Parousia did not occur, the church actually evolved from the eschatology of the realm in history toward the eschatology of transhistorical, supernatural perfection. In this evolution the specific essence of Christianity separated from its historical origin.[1] This separation began within the life of Jesus itself,[2] and it was on principle completed with the Pentecostal descent of the Spirit. Nevertheless, the expectation of an imminent coming of the realm was stirred to white heat again and again by the suffering of the persecutions; and the most grandiose expression of eschatological pathos, the Revelation of St. John, was included in the canon in spite of misgivings about its compatibility with the idea of the church. The inclusion had fateful consequences, for with the Revelation was accepted the revolutionary annunciation of the millennium in which Christ would reign with his saints on this earth.[3] Not only did the inclusion sanction the permanent effectiveness within Christianity of the broad mass of Jewish apocalyptic literature but it also raised the immediate question how chiliasm could be reconciled with idea and existence of the church. If Christianity consisted in the burning desire for deliverance from the world, if Christians lived in expectation of the end of unredeemed history, if their destiny could be fulfilled only by the realm in the sense of chapter 20 of Revelation, the church was

1. On the transition from eschatological to apocalyptic Christianity see Alois Dempf, *Sacrum Imperium* (Munich and Berlin, 1929), pp. 71 ff.

2. Albert Schweitzer, *Geschichte der Leben Jesu Forschung* (Tübingen, 1920), pp. 406 ff.; and Maurice Goguel, *Jésus* (2d ed.; Paris, 1950), the chapter on "La Crise galiléenne."

3. On the tension in early Christianity, the reception of Revelation, and its subsequent role in Western revolutionary eschatology see Jakob Taubes, *Abendländische Eschatologie* (Bern, 1947), esp. pp. 69 ff.

reduced to an ephemeral community of men waiting for the great event and hoping that it would occur in their lifetime. On the theoretical level the problem could be solved only by the tour de force of interpretation which St. Augustine performed in the *Civitas Dei*. There he roundly dismissed the literal belief in the millennium as "ridiculous fables" and then boldly declared the realm of the thousand years to be the reign of Christ in his church in the present saeculum that would continue until the Last Judgment and the advent of the eternal realm in the beyond.[4]

The Augustinian conception of the church, without substantial change, remained historically effective to the end of the Middle Ages. The revolutionary expectation of a Second Coming that would transfigure the structure of history on earth was ruled out as "ridiculous." The Logos had become flesh in Christ; the grace of redemption had been bestowed on man; there would be no divinization of society beyond the pneumatic presence of Christ in his church. Jewish chiliasm was excluded along with polytheism, just as Jewish monotheism had been excluded along with pagan, metaphysical monotheism. This left the church as the universal spiritual organization of saints and sinners who professed faith in Christ, as the representative of the *civitas Dei* in history, as the flash of eternity into time. And correspondingly it left the power organization of society as a temporal representation of man in the specific sense of a representation of that part of human nature that will pass away with the transfiguration of time into eternity. The one Christian society was articulated into its spiritual and temporal orders. In its temporal articulation it accepted the *conditio humana* without chiliastic fancies, while it heightened natural existence by the representation of spiritual destiny through the church.

This picture must be rounded out by remembering that the

4. Augustinus *Civitas Dei* xx. 7, 8, and 9.

idea of the temporal order was historically concretized through the Roman Empire. Rome was built into the idea of a Christian society by referring the Danielic prophecy of the Fourth Monarchy[5] to the *imperium sine fine*[6] as the last realm before the end of the world.[7] The church as the historically concrete representation of spiritual destiny was paralleled by the Roman Empire as the historically concrete representation of human temporality. Hence, the understanding of the medieval empire as the continuation of Rome was more than a vague historical hangover; it was part of a conception of history in which the end of Rome meant the end of the world in the eschatological sense. The conception survived in the realm of ideas for centuries while its basis of sentiments and institutions was crumbling away. The history of the world was constructed in the Augustinian tradition for the last time only by Bossuet, in his *Histoire universelle*, toward the end of the seventeenth century; and the first modern who dared to write a world history in direct opposition to Bossuet was Voltaire.

2

Western Christian society thus was articulated into the spiritual and temporal orders, with pope and emperor as the supreme representatives in both the existential and the transcendental sense. From this society with its established system of symbols emerge the specifically modern problems of representation, with the resurgence of the eschatology of the realm. The movement had a long social and intellectual prehistory, but the desire for a re-divinization of society produced a definite symbolism of its own only toward the end of the twelfth century. The analysis will start from the first clear and comprehensive expression of the idea in the person and work of Joachim of Flora.

5. Dan. 2:44.   6. Vergil *Aeneid* i. 278–79.

7. For the numerous sources see Ernst Troeltsch, *Die Soziallehren der christlichen Kirchen und Gruppen* (Tübingen, 1912), p. 112.

Joachim broke with the Augustinian conception of a Christian society when he applied the symbol of the Trinity to the course of history. In his speculation the history of mankind had three periods corresponding to the three persons of the Trinity. The first period of the world was the age of the Father; with the appearance of Christ began the age of the Son. But the age of the Son will not be the last one; it will be followed by a third age of the Spirit. The three ages were characterized as intelligible increases of spiritual fulfilment. The first age unfolded the life of the layman; the second age brought the active contemplative life of the priest; the third age would bring the perfect spiritual life of the monk. Moreover, the ages had comparable internal structures and a calculable length. From the comparison of structures it appeared that each age opened with a trinity of leading figures, that is, with two precursors, followed by the leader of the age himself; and from the calculation of length it followed that the age of the Son would reach its end in 1260. The leader of the first age was Abraham; the leader of the second age was Christ; and Joachim predicted that by 1260 there would appear the *Dux e Babylone*, the leader of the third age.[8]

In his trinitarian eschatology Joachim created the aggregate of symbols which govern the self-interpretation of modern political society to this day.

The first of these symbols is the conception of history as a sequence of three ages, of which the third age is intelligibly the final Third Realm. As variations of this symbol are recognizable the humanistic and encyclopedist periodization of history into ancient, medieval, and modern history; Turgot's and Comte's theory of a sequence of theological, metaphysical,

8. On Joachim of Flora see Herbert Grundmann, *Studien über Joachim von Floris* (Leipzig, 1927); Dempf, *op. cit.*, pp. 269 ff.; Ernesto Buonaiuti, *Gioacchino da Fiore* (Rome, 1931); the same author's "Introduction" to Joachim's *Tractatus super quatuor evangelia* (Rome, 1930); and the chapters on Joachim in Jakob Taubes' *Abendländische Eschatologie* and Karl Löwith's *Meaning in History* (Chicago, 1949).

and scientific phases; Hegel's dialectic of the three stages of freedom and self-reflective spiritual fulfilment; the Marxian dialectic of the three stages of primitive communism, class society, and final communism; and, finally, the National Socialist symbol of the Third Realm—though this is a special case requiring further attention.

The second symbol is that of the leader.[9] It had its immediate effectiveness in the movement of the Franciscan spirituals who saw in St. Francis the fulfilment of Joachim's prophecy; and its effectiveness was reinforced by Dante's speculation on the *Dux* of the new spiritual age. It then can be traced in the paracletic figures, the *homines spirituales* and *homines novi*, of the late Middle Ages, the Renaissance, and Reformation; it can be discerned as a component in Machiavelli's *principe;* and in the period of secularization it appears in the supermen of Condorcet, Comte, and Marx, until it dominates the contemporary scene through the paracletic leaders of the new realms.

The third symbol, sometimes blending into the second, is that of the prophet of the new age. In order to lend validity and conviction to the idea of a final Third Realm, the course of history as an intelligible, meaningful whole must be assumed accessible to human knowledge, either through a direct revelation or through speculative gnosis. Hence, the Gnostic prophet or, in the later stages of secularization, the Gnostic intellectual becomes an appurtenance of modern civilization. Joachim himself is the first instance of the species.

The fourth symbol is that of the brotherhood of autonomous persons. The third age of Joachim, by virtue of its new descent of the spirit, will transform men into members of the new realm without sacramental mediation of grace. In the third age the church will cease to exist because the charismatic gifts that are necessary for the perfect life will reach

9. For further transformations of Joachitism see Appendix I, "Modern Transfigurations of Joachism," in Löwith, *op. cit.*

men without administration of sacraments. While Joachim himself conceived the new age concretely as an order of monks, the idea of a community of the spiritually perfect who can live together without institutional authority was formulated on principle. The idea was capable of infinite variations. It can be traced in various degrees of purity in medieval and Renaissance sects, as well as in the Puritan churches of the saints; in its secularized form it has become a formidable component in the contemporary democratic creed; and it is the dynamic core in the Marxian mysticism of the realm of freedom and the withering-away of the state.

The National Socialist Third Realm is a special case. To be sure, Hitler's millennial prophecy authentically derives from Joachitic speculation, mediated in Germany through the Anabaptist wing of the Reformation and through the Johannine Christianity of Fichte, Hegel, and Schelling. Nevertheless, the concrete application of the trinitarian schema to the first German Reich that ended in 1806, the Bismarck Reich that ended in 1918, and the *Dritte Reich* of the National Socialist movement sounds flat and provincial if compared with the world-historical speculation of the German idealists, of Comte, or of Marx. This nationalist, accidental touch is due to the fact that the symbol of the *Dritte Reich* did not stem from the speculative effort of a philosopher of rank but rather from dubious literary transfers. The National Socialist propagandists picked it up from Moeller van den Bruck's tract of that name.[10] And Moeller, who had no National Socialist intentions, had found it as a convenient symbol in the course of his work on the German edition of Dostoevski. The Russian

10. Moeller van den Bruck, *Das Dritte Reich* (Hamburg, 1923). See also the chapter on "Das Dritte Reich und die Jungen Völker" in Moeller van den Bruck, *Die politischen Kräfte* (Breslau, 1933). The symbol gained acceptance slowly. The second edition of the *Dritte Reich* appeared only in 1930, five years after the author's death through suicide; see the "Introduction" by Mary Agnes Hamilton to the English edition, *Germany's Third Empire* (London, 1934).

idea of the Third Rome is characterized by the same blend of an eschatology of the spiritual realm with its realization by a political society as the National Socialist idea of the *Dritte Reich*. This other branch of political re-divinization must now be considered.

Only in the West was the Augustinian conception of the church historically effective to the point that it resulted in the clear double representation of society through the spiritual and temporal powers. The fact that the temporal ruler was situated at a considerable geographical distance from Rome certainly facilitated this evolution. In the East developed the Byzantine form of Caesaropapism, in direct continuity with the position of the emperor in pagan Rome. Constantinople was the Second Rome, as it appeared in the declaration of Justinian concerning the *consuetudo Romae:* "By Rome, however, must be understood not only the old one but also our royal city."[11] After the fall of Constantinople to the Turks, the idea of Moscow as the successor to the Orthodox empire gained ground in Russian clerical circles. Let me quote the famous passages from a letter of Filofei of Pskov to Ivan the Great:

The church of the first Rome fell because of the godless heresy of Apollinaris. The gates of the second Rome at Constantinople were smashed by the Ishmaelites. Today the holy apostolic church of the third Rome in thy Empire shines in the glory of Christian faith throughout the world. Know you, O pious Tsar, that all empires of the orthodox Christians have converged into thine own. You are the sole autocrat of the universe, the only tsar of all Christians. . . . According to the prophetic books all Christian empires have an end and

11. *Codex Justinianus* i. xvii. 1. 10. We are quoting the legal formalization of the idea. On the nuances of meaning with regard to the foundation and organization of Constantinople, in 330, see Andrew Alföldi, *The Conversion of Constantine and Pagan Rome*, trans. Harold Mattingly (Oxford, 1948), chap. ix: "The Old Rome and the New." The tension between the two Romes may be gathered from Canon 3 of the Council of Constantinople in 381: "The Bishop of Constantinople to have the primacy of honor next after the Bishop of Rome, because that Constantinople is New Rome" (Henry Bettenson, *Documents of the Christian Church* [New York, 1947], p. 115).

will converge into one empire, that of our gossudar, that is, into the Empire of Russia. Two Romes have fallen, but the third will last, and there will not be a fourth one.[12]

It took about a century to institutionalize the idea. Ivan IV was the first Rurikide to have himself crowned, in 1547, as czar of the Orthodox;[13] and in 1589 the patriarch of Constantinople was compelled to institute the first autocephalous patriarch of Moscow, now with the official recognition of Moscow as the Third Rome.[14]

The dates of rise and institutionalization of the idea are of importance. The reign of Ivan the Great coincides with the consolidation of the Western national states (England, France, and Spain), and the reigns of Ivan IV and of Theodore I coincide with the Western Reformation. Precisely at the time when the Western imperial articulation ultimately disintegrated, when Western society rearticulated itself into the nations and the plurality of churches, Russia entered on her career as the heir of Rome. From her very beginnings Russia was not a nation in the Western sense but a civilizational area, dominated ethnically by the Great Russians and formed into a political society by the symbolism of Roman continuation.

That Russian society was in a class by itself was gradually recognized by the West. In 1488 Maximilian I still tried to integrate Russia into the Western political system by offering a royal crown to Ivan the Great. The Grand Duke of Moscow refused the honor on the grounds that his authority stemmed from his ancestors, that it had the blessing of God, and, hence,

---

12. On the Third Rome see Hildegard Schaeder, *Moskau—Das Dritte Rom: Studien zur Geschichte der politischen Theorien in der slavischen Welt* (Hamburg, 1929); Joseph Olšr, *Gli ultimi Rurikidi e le base ideologiche della sovranità dello stato Russo* ("Orientalia Christiana," Vol. XII [Rome, 1946]); Hugo Rahner, *Vom Ersten bis zum Dritten Rom* (Innsbruck, 1950); Paul Miliukov, *Outlines of Russian Culture*, Part I: *Religion and the Church* (Philadelphia, 1945), pp. 15 ff.

13. George Vernadsky, *Political and Diplomatic History of Russia* (Boston, 1936), p. 158.

14. *Ibid.*, p. 180.

that there was no need of confirmation from the Western emperor.[15] A century later, in 1576, at the time of the Western wars with the Turks, Maximilian II went a step further by offering Ivan IV recognition as the emperor of the Greek East in return for assistance.[16] Again the Russian ruler was not interested even in an imperial crown, for, at that time, Ivan was already engaged in building the Russian Empire through the liquidation of the feudal nobility and its replacement by the *oprichnina*, the new service nobility.[17] Through this bloody operation Ivan the Terrible stamped on Russia the indelible social articulation which has determined her inner political history to this day. Transcendentally Russia was distinguished from all Western nations as the imperial representative of Christian truth; and through her social rearticulation, from which the czar emerged as the existential representative, she was radically cut off from the development of representative institutions in the sense of the Western national states. Napoleon, finally, recognized the Russian problem when, in 1802, he said that there were only two nations in the world: Russia and the Occident.[18]

Russia developed a type *sui generis* of representation, in both the transcendental and the existential respects. The Westernization since Peter the Great did not change the type fundamentally because it had practically no effect with regard to social articulation. One can speak, indeed, of a personal Westernization in the ranks of the high nobility, in the wake of the Napoleonic Wars, in the generation of Chaadaev, Gagarin, and Pecherin; but the individual servants of the czar did not transform themselves into an estate of the nobility, into an articulate *baronagium*. Perhaps the necessity of co-operative class action as the condition of a political Westernization of

15. *Ibid.*, p. 149.   16. Rahner, *op. cit.*, p. 15.
17. Vernadsky, *op. cit.*, pp. 169 ff.
18. Napoleon, *Vues politiques* (Rio de Janeiro, *s.a.*), p. 340.

Russia was not even seen; and certainly, if the possibility for an evolution in this direction ever existed, it was finished with the Dekabrist revolt of 1825. Immediately afterward, with Khomyakov, began the Slavophilic, anti-Western philosophy of history which enhanced the apocalypse of the Third Rome, with broad effectiveness in the intelligentsia of the middle nobility, into the messianic, eschatological mission of Russia for mankind. In Dostoevski this superimposition of messianism crystallized in the curiously ambivalent vision of an autocratic, orthodox Russia that somehow would conquer the world and in this conquest blossom out into the free society of all Christians in the true faith.[19] It is the ambivalent vision which, in its secularized form, inspires a Russian dictatorship of the proletariat that in its conquest of the world will blossom out into the Marxian realm of freedom. The tentative Western articulation of Russian society under the liberal czars has become an episode of the past with the revolution of 1917. The people as a whole have become again the servants of the czar in the old Muscovite sense, with the cadres of the Communist party as its service nobility; the *oprichnina* which Ivan the Terrible had established on the basis of an agricultural economy was re-established with a vengeance on the basis of an industrial economy.[20]

3

From the exposition of Joachitic symbols, from the cursory survey of their later variants, and from their blending with the political apocalypse of the Third Rome, it will have become clear that the new eschatology decisively affects the structure of modern politics. It has produced a well-circum-

19. For this view of Dostoevski see Dmitri Merezhkovski, *Die religiöse Revolution* (printed as Introduction to Dostoevski's *Politische Schriften* [Munich, 1920]), and Bernhard Schultze, *Russische Denker* (Wien, 1950), pp. 125 ff.

20. Alexander von Schelting, *Russland und Europa* (Bern, 1948), pp. 123 ff. and 261 ff.

scribed symbolism by means of which Western political societies interpret the meaning of their existence; and the adherents of one or the other of the variants determine the articulation of society domestically as well as on the world scene. Up to this point, however, the symbolism has been accepted on the level of self-interpretation and described as a historical phenomenon. It must now be submitted to critical analysis of its principal aspects, and the foundation for this analysis must be laid through a formulation of the theoretically relevant issue.

The Joachitic eschatology is, by its subject matter, a speculation on the meaning of history. In order to determine its specific difference, it must be set off against the Christian philosophy of history that was traditional at the time, that is, against Augustinian speculation. Into the traditional speculation had entered the Jewish-Christian idea of an end of history in the sense of an intelligible state of perfection. History no longer moved in cycles, as it did with Plato and Aristotle, but acquired direction and destination. Beyond Jewish messianism in the strict sense the specifically Christian conception of history had, then, advanced toward the understanding of the end as a transcendental fulfilment. In his elaboration of this theoretical insight St. Augustine distinguished between a profane sphere of history in which empires rise and fall and a sacred history which culminates in the appearance of Christ and the establishment of the church. He, furthermore, imbedded sacred history in a transcendental history of the *civitas Dei* which includes the events in the angelic sphere as well as the transcendental eternal sabbath. Only transcendental history, including the earthly pilgrimage of the church, has direction toward its eschatological fulfilment. Profane history, on the other hand, has no such direction; it is a waiting for the end; its present mode of being is that of a *saeculum senescens*, of an age that grows old.[21]

21. For an account of the Augustinian conception of history see Löwith, *op. cit.*

By the time of Joachim, Western civilization was strongly growing; and an age that began to feel its muscles would not easily bear the Augustinian defeatism with regard to the mundane sphere of existence. The Joachitic speculation was an attempt to endow the immanent course of history with a meaning that was not provided in the Augustinian conception. And for this purpose Joachim used what he had at hand, that is, the meaning of transcendental history. In this first Western attempt at an immanentization of meaning the connection with Christianity was not lost. The new age of Joachim would bring an increase of fulfilment within history, but the increase would not be due to an immanent eruption; it would come through a new transcendental irruption of the spirit. The idea of a radically immanent fulfilment grew rather slowly, in a long process that roughly may be called "from humanism to enlightenment"; only in the eighteenth century, with the idea of progress, had the increase of meaning in history become a completely intramundane phenomenon, without transcendental irruptions. This second phase of immanentization shall be called "secularization."

From the Joachitic immanentization a theoretical problem arises which occurs neither in classic antiquity nor in orthodox Christianity, that is, the problem of an eidos of history.[22] In Hellenic speculation, to be sure, we also have a problem of essence in politics; the polis has an eidos both for Plato and for Aristotle. But the actualization of this essence is governed by the rhythm of growth and decay, and the rhythmical embodiment and disembodiment of essence in political reality is the mystery of existence; it is not an additional eidos. The soteriological truth of Christianity, then, breaks with the rhythm of existence; beyond temporal successes and reverses lies the supernatural destiny of man, the perfection through grace in the beyond. Man and mankind now have fulfilment,

22. On the eidos of history see Hans Urs von Balthasar, *Theologie der Geschichte* (Einsiedeln, 1950), and Löwith, *op. cit.*, *passim*.

but it lies beyond nature. Again there is no eidos of history, because the eschatological supernature is not a nature in the philosophical, immanent sense. The problem of an eidos in history, hence, arises only when Christian transcendental fulfilment becomes immanentized. Such an immanentist hypostasis of the eschaton, however, is a theoretical fallacy. Things are not things, nor do they have essences, by arbitrary declaration. The course of history as a whole is no object of experience; history has no eidos, because the course of history extends into the unknown future. The meaning of history, thus, is an illusion; and this illusionary eidos is created by treating a symbol of faith as if it were a proposition concerning an object of immanent experience.

The fallacious character of an eidos of history has been shown on principle—but the analysis can and must be carried one step further into certain details. The Christian symbolism of supernatural destination has in itself a theoretical structure, and this structure is continued into the variants of immanentization. The pilgrim's progress, the sanctification of life, is a movement toward a telos, a goal; and this goal, the beatific vision, is a state of perfection. Hence, in the Christian symbolism one can distinguish the movement as its teleological component, from a state of highest value as the axiological component.[23] The two components reappear in the variants of immanentization; and they can accordingly be classified as variants which either accentuate the teleological or the axiological component or combine them both in their symbolism. In the first case, when the accent lies strongly on movement, without clarity about final perfection, the result will be the progressivist interpretation of history. The aim need not be clarified because progressivist thinkers, men like

23. For the distinction of the two components (which was introduced by Troeltsch) and the ensuing theological debate see Hans Urs von Balthasar, *Prometheus* (Heidelberg, 1947), pp. 12 ff.

Diderot or D'Alembert, assume a selection of desirable factors as the standard and interpret progress as qualitative and quantitative increase of the present good—the "bigger and better" of our simplifying slogan. This is a conservative attitude, and it may become reactionary unless the original standard be adjusted to the changing historical situation. In the second case, when the accent lies strongly on the state of perfection, without clarity about the means that are required for its realization, the result will be utopianism. It may assume the form of an axiological dream world, as in the utopia of More, when the thinker is still aware that and why the dream is unrealizable; or, with increasing theoretical illiteracy, it may assume the form of various social idealisms, such as the abolition of war, of unequal distribution of property, of fear and want. And, finally, immanentization may extend to the complete Christian symbol. The result will then be the active mysticism of a state of perfection, to be achieved through a revolutionary transfiguration of the nature of man, as, for instance, in Marxism.

4

The analysis can now be resumed on the level of principle. The attempt at constructing an eidos of history will lead into the fallacious immanentization of the Christian eschaton. The understanding of the attempt as fallacious, however, raises baffling questions with regard to the type of man who will indulge in it. The fallacy looks rather elemental. Can it be assumed that the thinkers who indulged in it were not intelligent enough to penetrate it? Or that they penetrated it but propagated it nevertheless for some obscure evil reason? The mere asking of such questions carries their negation. Obviously one cannot explain seven centuries of intellectual history by stupidity and dishonesty. A drive must rather be assumed in the souls of these men which blinded them to the fallacy.

The nature of this drive cannot be discovered by submitting the structure of the fallacy to an even closer analysis. The attention must rather concentrate on what the thinkers achieved by their fallacious construction. On this point there is no doubt. They achieved a certainty about the meaning of history, and about their own place in it, which otherwise they would not have had. Certainties, now, are in demand for the purpose of overcoming uncertainties with their accompaniment of anxiety; and the next question then would be: What specific uncertainty was so disturbing that it had to be overcome by the dubious means of fallacious immanentization? One does not have to look far afield for an answer. Uncertainty is the very essence of Christianity. The feeling of security in a "world full of gods" is lost with the gods themselves; when the world is de-divinized, communication with the world-transcendent God is reduced to the tenuous bond of faith, in the sense of Heb. 11:1, as the substance of things hoped for and the proof of things unseen. Ontologically, the substance of things hoped for is nowhere to be found but in faith itself; and, epistemologically, there is no proof for things unseen but again this very faith.[24] The bond is tenuous, indeed, and it may snap easily. The life of the soul in openness toward God, the waiting, the periods of aridity and dulness, guilt and despondency, contrition and repentance, forsakenness and hope against hope, the silent stirrings of love and grace, trembling on the verge of a certainty which if gained is loss—the very lightness of this fabric may prove too heavy a burden for men who lust for massively possessive experience. The danger of a breakdown of faith to a socially relevant degree, now, will increase in the measure in which Christianity is a worldly success, that is, it will grow when Christianity penetrates a

24. Our reflections on the uncertainty of faith must be understood as a psychology of experience. For the theology of the definition of faith in Heb. 11:1, which is presupposed in our analysis, see Thomas Aquinas *Summa theologica* ii-ii. Q. 4, Art. 1.

civilizational area thoroughly, supported by institutional pressure, and when, at the same time, it undergoes an internal process of spiritualization, of a more complete realization of its essence. The more people are drawn or pressured into the Christian orbit, the greater will be the number among them who do not have the spiritual stamina for the heroic adventure of the soul that is Christianity; and the likeliness of a fall from faith will increase when civilizational progress of education, literacy, and intellectual debate will bring the full seriousness of Christianity to the understanding of ever more individuals. Both of these processes characterized the high Middle Ages. The historical detail is not the present concern; it will be sufficient to refer summarily to the growing town societies with their intense spiritual culture as the primary centers from which the danger radiated into Western society at large.

If the predicament of a fall from faith in the Christian sense occurs as a mass phenomenon, the consequences will depend on the content of the civilizational environment into which the agnostics are falling. A man cannot fall back on himself in an absolute sense, because, if he tried, he would find very soon that he has fallen into the abyss of his despair and nothingness; he will have to fall back on a less differentiated culture of spiritual experience. Under the civilizational conditions of the twelfth century it was impossible to fall back into Greco-Roman polytheism, because it had disappeared as the living culture of a society; and the stunted remnants could hardly be revived, because they had lost their spell precisely for men who had tasted of Christianity. The fall could be caught only by experiential alternatives, sufficiently close to the experience of faith that only a discerning eye would see the difference, but receding far enough from it to remedy the uncertainty of faith in the strict sense. Such alternative experiences were at hand in the gnosis which had accompanied Christianity from its very beginnings.[25]

The economy of this lecture does not allow a description of the gnosis of antiquity or of the history of its transmission into the Western Middle Ages; enough to say that at the time gnosis was a living religious culture on which men could fall back. The attempt at immanentizing the meaning of existence is fundamentally an attempt at bringing our knowledge of transcendence into a firmer grip than the *cognitio fidei*, the cognition of faith, will afford; and Gnostic experiences offer this firmer grip in so far as they are an expansion of the soul to the point where God is drawn into the existence of man. This expansion will engage the various human faculties; and, hence, it is possible to distinguish a range of Gnostic varieties according to the faculty which predominates in the operation of getting this grip on God. Gnosis may be primarily intellectual and assume the form of speculative penetration of the mystery of creation and existence, as, for instance, in the contemplative gnosis of Hegel or Schelling. Or it may be primarily emotional and assume the form of an indwelling of divine substance in the human soul, as, for instance, in paracletic sectarian leaders. Or it may be primarily volitional and assume the form of activist redemption of man and society, as in the instance of revolutionary activists like Comte, Marx, or Hitler. These Gnostic experiences, in the amplitude of their variety, are the core of the redivinization of society, for the men who fall into these experiences divinize themselves by substituting more massive modes of participation in divinity for faith in the Christian sense.[26]

25. The exploration of gnosis is so rapidly advancing that only a study of the principal works of the last generation will mediate an understanding of its dimensions. Of special value are Eugène de Faye, *Gnostiques et gnosticisme* (2d ed.; Paris, 1925); Hans Jonas, *Gnosis und spätantiker Geist* (Götingen, 1934); Simone Pétrement, *Le Dualisme chez Platon, les Gnostiques et les Manichéens* (Paris, 1947); and Hans Söderberg, *La Religion des Cathares* (Uppsala, 1949).

26. For a general suggestion concerning the range of Gnostic phenomena in the modern world see Balthasar, *Prometheus*, p. 6.

A clear understanding of these experiences as the active core of immanentist eschatology is necessary, because otherwise the inner logic of the Western political development from medieval immanentism through humanism, enlightenment, progressivism, liberalism, positivism, into Marxism will be obscured. The intellectual symbols developed by the various types of immanentists will frequently be in conflict with one another, and the various types of Gnostics will oppose one another. One can easily imagine how indignant a humanistic liberal will be when he is told that his particular type of immanentism is one step on the road to Marxism. It will not be superfluous, therefore, to recall the principle that the substance of history is to be found on the level of experiences, not on the level of ideas. Secularism could be defined as a radicalization of the earlier forms of paracletic immanentism, because the experiential divinization of man is more radical in the secularist case. Feuerbach and Marx, for instance, interpreted the transcendent God as the projection of what is best in man into a hypostatic beyond; for them the great turning point of history, therefore, would come when man draws his projection back into himself, when he becomes conscious that he himself is God, when as a consequence man is transfigured into superman.[27] This Marxian transfiguration does, indeed, carry to its extreme a less radical medieval experience which draws the spirit of God into man, while leaving God himself in his transcendence. The superman marks the end of a road on which we find such figures as the "godded man" of English Reformation mystics.[28] These considerations, moreover, will explain and justify the earlier warning against characterizing modern political movements as neopagan. Gnostic experiences

27. On the superman of Feuerbach and Marx see Henri de Lubac, *Le Drame de l'humanisme athée* (3d ed.; Paris, 1945), pp. 15 ff.; Löwith, *op. cit.*, especially the quotation on p. 36 concerning the "new men"; and Eric Voegelin, "The Formation of the Marxian Revolutionary Idea" *Review of Politics*, Vol. XII (1950).

28. The "godded man" is a term of Henry Nicholas (see Rufus M. Jones, *Studies in Mystical Religion* [London, 1936], p. 434).

determine a structure of political reality that is *sui generis*. A line of gradual transformation connects medieval with contemporary gnosticism. And the transformation is so gradual, indeed, that it would be difficult to decide whether contemporary phenomena should be classified as Christian because they are intelligibly an outgrowth of Christian heresies of the Middle Ages or whether medievel phenomena should be classified as anti-Christian because they are intelligibly the origin of modern anti-Christianism. The best course will be to drop such questions and to recognize the essence of modernity as the growth of gnosticism.

Gnosis was an accompaniment of Christianity from its very beginnings; its traces are to be found in St. Paul and St. John.[29] Gnostic heresy was the great opponent of Christianity in the early centuries; and Irenaeus surveyed and criticized the manifold of its variants in his *Adversus Haereses* (*ca.* 180)—a standard treatise on the subject that still will be consulted with profit by the student who wants to understand modern political ideas and movements. Moreover, besides the Christian there also existed a Jewish, a pagan, and an Islamic gnosis; and quite possibly the common origin of all these branches of gnosis will have to be sought in the basic experiential type that prevailed in the pre-Christian area of Syriac civilization. Nowhere, however, has gnosis assumed the form of speculation on the meaning of immanent history as it did in the high Middle Ages; gnosis does not by inner necessity lead to the fallacious construction of history which characterizes modernity since Joachim. Hence, in the drive for certainty there must be contained a further component which bends gnosis specifically toward historical speculation. This further component is the civilizational expansiveness of Western society in the high Middle Ages. It is a coming-of-age in search of its

---

29. On gnosis in early Christianity see Rudolf Bultmann, *Das Urchristentum im Rahmen der antiken Religionen* (Zurich, 1949).

meaning, a conscious growth that will not put up with the interpretation as senescence. And, in fact, the self-endowment of Western civilization with meaning closely followed the actual expansion and differentiation. The spiritual growth of the West through the orders since Cluny expressed itself, in Joachim's speculation in the idea of a Third Realm of the monks; the early philosophical and literary humanism expressed itself in Dante's and Petrarch's idea of an Apollinian Imperium, a Third Realm of intellectual life that succeeds the imperial spiritual and temporal orders;[30] and in the Age of Reason a Condorcet conceived the idea of a unified civilization of mankind in which everybody would be a French intellectual.[31] The social carriers of the movements, in their turn, changed with the differentiation and articulation of Western society. In the early phases of modernity they were the townspeople and peasants in opposition to feudal society; in the later phases they were the progressive bourgeoisie, the socialist workers, and the Fascist lower middle class. And, finally, with the prodigious advancement of science since the seventeenth century, the new instrument of cognition would become, one is inclined to say inevitably, the symbolic vehicle of Gnostic truth. In the Gnostic speculation of scientism this particular variant reached its extreme when the positivist perfector of science replaced the era of Christ by the era of Comte. Scientism has remained to this day one of the strongest Gnostic movements in Western society; and the immanentist pride in science is so strong that even the special sciences have each left a distinguishable sediment in the variants of salvation through physics, economics, sociology, biology, and psychology.

30. On the Apollinian Imperium as a Third Realm see Karl Burdach, *Reformation, Renaissance, Humanismus* (2d ed.; Berlin and Leipzig, 1926), pp. 133 ff.; and the same author's *Rienzo und die geistige Wandlung seiner Zeit* (Berlin, 1913–28), Vol. II/I: *Vom Mittelalter zur Reformation*, p. 542.

31. Condorcet, *Esquisse* (1795), pp. 310–18.

5

This analysis of the components in modern Gnostic speculation does not claim to be exhaustive, but it has been carried
far enough for the more immediate purpose of elucidating the
experiences which determine the political articulation of
Western society under the symbolism of the Third Realm.
There emerges the image of a society, identifiable and intelligible as a unit by its evolution as the representative of a historically unique type of Gnostic truth. Following the Aristotelian procedure, the analysis started from the self-interpretation of society by means of the Joachitic symbols of the
twelfth century. Now that their meaning has been clarified
through theoretical understanding, a date can be assigned to
the beginning of this civilizational course. A suitable date for
its formal beginning would be the activation of ancient gnosticism through Scotus Eriugena in the ninth century, because
his works, as well as those of Dionysius Areopagita which he
translated, were a continuous influence in the underground
Gnostic sects before they came to the surface in the twelfth
and thirteenth centuries.

This is a long course of a thousand years, long enough to
have aroused reflections on its decline and end. These reflections on Western society as a civilizational course that comes
into view as a whole because it is moving intelligibly toward
an end have raised one of the thorniest questions to plague the
student of Western politics. On the one hand, as you know,
there begins in the eighteenth century a continuous stream of
literature on the decline of Western civilization; and, whatever misgivings one may entertain on this or that special argument, one cannot deny that the theorists of decline on the
whole have a case. On the other hand, the same period is characterized, if by anything, by an exuberantly expansive vitality
in the sciences, in technology, in the material control of en-

vironment, in the increase of population, of the standard of living, of health and comfort, of mass education, of social consciousness and responsibility; and again, whatever misgivings one may entertain with regard to this or that item on the list, one cannot deny that the progressivists have a case, too. This conflict of interpretations leaves in its wake the adumbrated thorny question, that is, the question how a civilization can advance and decline at the same time. A consideration of this question suggests itself, because it seems possible that the analysis of modern gnosticism will furnish at least a partial solution of the problem.

Gnostic speculation overcame the uncertainty of faith by receding from transcendence and endowing man and his intramundane range of action with the meaning of eschatological fulfilment. In the measure in which this immanentization progressed experientially, civilizational activity became a mystical work of self-salvation. The spiritual strength of the soul which in Christianity was devoted to the sanctification of life could now be diverted into the more appealing, more tangible, and, above all, so much easier creation of the terrestrial paradise. Civilizational action became a *divertissement*, in the sense of Pascal, but a *divertissement* which demonically absorbed into itself the eternal destiny of man and substituted for the life of the spirit. Nietzsche most tersely expressed the nature of this demonic diversion when he raised the question why anyone should live in the embarrassing condition of a being in need of the love and grace of God. "Love yourself through grace—was his solution—then you are no longer in need of your God, and you can act the whole drama of Fall and Redemption to its end in yourself."[32] And how can this miracle be achieved, this miracle of self-salvation, and how this redemption by extending grace to yourself? The great historical answer was given by the successive types of Gnostic action that have made

32. Nietzsche, *Morgenröthe*, § 79.

modern civilization what it is. The miracle was worked successively through the literary and artistic achievement which secured the immortality of fame for the humanistic intellectual, through the discipline and economic success which certified salvation to the Puritan saint, through the civilizational contributions of the liberals and progressives, and, finally, through the revolutionary action that will establish the Communist or some other Gnostic millennium. Gnosticism, thus, most effectively released human forces for the building of a civilization because on their fervent application to intramundane activity was put the premium of salvation. The historical result was stupendous. The resources of man that came to light under such pressure were in themselves a revelation, and their application to civilizational work produced the truly magnificent spectacle of Western progressive society. However fatuous the surface arguments may be, the widespread belief that modern civilization is Civilization in a pre-eminent sense is experientially justified; the endowment with the meaning of salvation has made the rise of the West, indeed, an apocalypse of civilization.

On this apocalyptic spectacle, however, falls a shadow; for the brilliant expansion is accompanied by a danger that grows apace with progress. The nature of this danger became apparent in the form which the idea of immanent salvation assumed in the gnosticism of Comte. The founder of positivism institutionalized the premium on civilizational contributions in so far as he guaranteed immortality through preservation of the contributor and his deeds in the memory of mankind. There were provided honorific degrees of such immortality, and the highest honor would be the reception of the meritorious contributor into the calendar of positivistic saints. But what should in this order of things become of men who would rather follow God than the new Augustus Comte? Such miscreants who were not inclined to make their social contributions according to Comtean standards would simply be committed to the hell of social oblivion. The idea deserves attention. Here is a Gnostic paraclete setting himself up as the world-immanent Last Judgment of mankind, deciding on immortality or annihilation for every human being. The material civilization of the West, to be sure, is still advancing; but on this rising plane of civilization the progressive symbolism of contributions, commemoration, and oblivion draws the contours of those "holes of oblivion" into which the divine redeemers of the Gnostic empires drop their victims with a bullet in the neck. This end of progress was not contemplated in the halcyon days of Gnostic exuberance. Milton released Adam and Eve with "a paradise within them, happier far" than the Paradise lost; when they went forth, "the world was all before them"; and they were cheered "with meditation on the happy end." But when historically man goes forth, with the Gnostic "Paradise within him," and when he penetrates into the world before him, there is little cheer in meditation on the not so happy end.

The death of the spirit is the price of progress. Nietzsche revealed this mystery of the Western apocalypse when he announced that God was dead and that He had been murdered.[33] This Gnostic murder is constantly committed by the men who sacrifice God to civilization. The more fervently all human energies are thrown into the great enterprise of salvation through world-immanent action, the farther the human beings who engage in this enterprise move away from the life of the spirit. And since the life of the spirit is the source of order in man and society, the very success of a Gnostic civilization is the cause of its decline.

33. On the "murder of God" passages in Nietzsche, prehistory of the idea, and literary debate see Lubac, *op. cit.*, pp. 40 ff. For the most comprehensive exposition of the idea in Nietzsche's work see Karl Jaspers, *Nietzsche: Einführung in das Verständnis seines Philosophierens* (Berlin and Leipzig, 1936), under the references in the register.

A civilization can, indeed, advance and decline at the same time—but not forever. There is a limit toward which this ambiguous process moves; the limit is reached when an activist sect which represents the Gnostic truth organizes the civilization into an empire under its rule. Totalitarianism, defined as the existential rule of Gnostic activists, is the end form of progressive civilization.

V

GNOSTIC REVOLUTION—THE PURITAN CASE

✻

1

THE analysis of Gnostic experiences has resulted in a concept of modernity that seems to be at variance with the conventional meaning of the term. Conventionally, Western history is divided into periods with a formal incision around 1500, the later period being the modern phase of Western society. If, however, modernity is defined as the growth of gnosticism, beginning perhaps as early as the ninth century, it becomes a process within Western society extending deeply into its medieval period. Hence, the conception of a succession of phases would have to be replaced by that of a continuous evolution in which modern gnosticism rises victoriously to predominance over a civilizational tradition deriving from the Mediterranean discoveries of anthropological and soteriological truth. This new conception in itself does no more than reflect the present state of empirical historiography and, therefore, is not in need of further justification. Nevertheless, there remains the question whether the conventional periodization has no bearing at all on the issue of gnosticism; for it would be surprising, indeed, if a symbol that has gained such wide acceptance in the self-interpretation of Western society were not in some way connected with the fundamental problem of representation of truth.

In fact, such a connection exists. The conception of a modern age succeeding the Middle Ages is itself one of the symbols created by the Gnostic movement. It belongs in the class of the Third Realm symbols. Ever since, in the fifteenth century,

Biondo treated the millennium from the fall of Rome in 410 to the year 1410 as a closed age of the past, the symbol of a new, modern age has been used by the successive waves of humanistic, Protestant, and enlightened intellectuals for expressing their consciousness of being the representatives of a new truth. Precisely, however, because the world, under the guidance of the Gnostics, is being renewed at frequent intervals, it is impossible to arrive at a critically justified periodization while listening to their claims. By the immanent logic of its own theological symbolism each of the Gnostic waves has as good a claim to consider itself the great wave of the future as any other. There is no reason why a modern period should begin with humanism rather than with the Reformation, or with Enlightenment rather than with Marxism. Hence, the problem cannot be solved on the level of Gnostic symbolism. We must descend to the level of existential representation in order to find a motive for periodization; for an epoch would be marked indeed if, in the struggle for existential representation, there existed a decisive revolutionary victory of gnosticism over the forces of Western tradition. If the question is stated in such terms, the conventional periodization becomes meaningful. While none of the movements deserves preference by the content of its truth, a clear epoch in Western history is marked by the Reformation, understood as the successful invasion of Western institutions by Gnostic movements. The movements which hitherto existed in a socially marginal position—tolerated, suppressed, or underground—erupted in the Reformation with unexpected strength on a broad front, with the result of splitting the universal church and embarking on their gradual conquest of the political institutions in the national states.

The revolutionary eruption of the Gnostic movements affected existential representation throughout Western society. The event is so vast in dimensions that no survey even of its general characteristics can be attempted in the present lectures. In order to convey an understanding of at least some of the more important traits of the Gnostic revolution, it will be best to concentrate the analysis on a specific national area and on a specific phase within it. Certain aspects of the Puritan impact on the English public order will be the most suitable subject for a brief study. Moreover, this selection suggests itself because the English sixteenth century had the rare good fortune of a brilliant observer of the Gnostic movement in the person of the "judicious Hooker." In the Preface of his *Ecclesiastical Polity* Hooker gave an astute type study of the Puritan, as well as of the psychological mechanism by which Gnostic mass movements operate. These pages are an invaluable asset for the student of the Gnostic revolution; the present analysis will, therefore, properly begin with a summary of Hooker's portrait of the Puritan.

2

In order to start a movement moving, there must in the first place be somebody who has a "cause." From the context in Hooker it appears that the term "cause" was of recent usage in politics and that probably the Puritans had invented this formidable weapon of the Gnostic revolutionaries. In order to advance his "cause," the man who has it will, "in the hearing of the multitude," indulge in severe criticisms of social evils and in particular of the conduct of the upper classes. Frequent repetition of the performance will induce the opinion among the hearers that the speakers must be men of singular integrity, zeal, and holiness, for only men who are singularly good can be so deeply offended by evil. The next step will be the concentration of popular ill-will on the established government. This task can be psychologically performed by attributing all fault and corruption, as it exists in the world because of human frailty, to the action or inaction of the government. By such imputation of evil to a specific institution the speakers prove their wisdom to the multitude of men who by themselves would never have thought of such a connection; and at the same time they show the point that must be attacked if evil shall be removed from this world. After such preparation, the time will be ripe for recommending a new form of government as the "sovereign remedy of all evils." For people who are "possessed with dislike and discontentment at things present" are crazed enough to "imagine that any thing (the virtue whereof they hear recommended) would help them; but the most, which they least have tried."

If a movement, like the Puritan, relies on the authority of a literary source, the leaders will then have to fashion "the very notions and conceits of men's minds in such a sort" that the followers will automatically associate scriptural passages and terms with their doctrine, however ill founded the association may be, and that with equal automatism they will be blind to the content of Scripture that is incompatible with their doctrine. Next comes the decisive step in consolidating a Gnostic attitude, that is, "the persuading of men credulous and over-capable of such pleasing errors, that it is the special illumination of the Holy Ghost, whereby they discern those things in the word, which others reading yet discern them not." They will experience themselves as the elect; and this experience breeds "high terms of separation between such and the rest of the world"; so that, as a consequence, mankind will be divided into the "brethren" and the "worldlings."

When Gnostic experience is consolidated, the social raw material is ready for existential representation by a leader. For, Hooker continues, such people will prefer each other's company to that of the rest of the world, they will voluntarily accept counsel and direction from the indoctrinators, they will neglect their own affairs and devote excessive time to service of the cause, and they will extend generous material aid to the leaders of the movement. An especially important function in the formation of such societies will have women, because they are weak in judgment, emotionally more accessible, tactically well placed to influence husbands, children, servants, and friends, more inclined than men to serve as a kind of intelligence officers concerning the state of affections in their circle, and more liberal in financial aid.

Once a social environment of this type is organized, it will be difficult, if not impossible, to break it up by persuasion. "Let any man of contrary opinion open his mouth to persuade them, they close up their ears, his reasons they weight not, all is answered with rehearsal of the words of John: 'We are of God; he that knoweth God heareth us': as for the rest ye are of the world: for this world's pomp and vanity it is that ye speak, and the world, whose ye are, heareth you." They are impermeable to argument and have their answers well drilled. Suggest to them that they are unable to judge in such matters, and they will answer, "God hath chosen the simple." Show them convincingly that they are talking nonsense, and you will hear "Christ's own apostle was accounted mad." Try the meekest warning of discipline, and they will be profuse on "the cruelty of bloodthirsty men" and cast themselves in the role of "innocency persecuted for the truth." In brief: the attitude is psychologically iron-clad and beyond shaking by argument.[1]

3

Hooker's description of the Puritan so clearly applies also to later types of Gnostic revolutionaries that the point need not be labored. From his analysis, however, an issue emerges which deserves closer attention. The portrait of the Puritan resulted from a clash between gnosticism, on the one side, and the classic and Christian tradition represented by Hooker, on the other side. It was drawn by a thinker of considerable intel-

1. Richard Hooker, *Works*, ed. Keble (7th ed.; Oxford, 1888). The summary covers *ibid.*, I, 145–55.

lectual qualities and erudition. The argument would, therefore, inevitably turn on the issue which in more recent treat-
ments of Puritanism has been so badly neglected, that is, on
the intellectual defects of the Gnostic position which are apt
to destroy the universe of rational discourse as well as the social function of persuasion. Hooker discerned that the Puritan
position was not based on Scripture but was a "cause" of a
vastly different origin. It would use Scripture when passages
torn out of context would support the cause, and for the rest it
would blandly ignore Scripture as well as the traditions and
rules of interpretation that had been developed by fifteen centuries of Christianity. In the early phases of the Gnostic revolution this camouflage was necessary—neither could an openly
anti-Christian movement have been socially successful, nor
had gnosticism in fact moved so far away from Christianity
that its carriers were conscious of the direction in which they
were moving. Nevertheless, the distance was already large
enough to make the camouflage embarrassing in the face of
competent criticism. In order to ward off this embarrassment,
two technical devices were developed which to this day have
remained the great instruments of Gnostic revolution.

In order to make the scriptural camouflage effective, the
selections from Scripture, as well as the interpretation put
upon them, had to be standardized. Real freedom of scriptural
interpretation for everybody according to his preferences and
state of education would have resulted in the chaotic conditions which characterized the early years of the Reformation;
moreover, if one interpretation was admitted to be as good as
another, there was no case against the tradition of the church,
which, after all, was based on an interpretation of Scripture,
too. From this dilemma between chaos and tradition emerged
the first device, that is, the systematic formulation of the new
doctrine in scriptural terms, as it was provided by Calvin's
Institutes. A work of this type would serve the double purpose

of a guide to the right reading of Scripture and of an authentic formulation of truth that would make recourse to earlier literature unnecessary. For the designation of this genus of Gnostic literature a technical term is needed; since the study of Gnostic phenomena is too recent to have developed one, the Arabic term *koran* will have to do for the present. The work of Calvin, thus, may be called the first deliberately created Gnostic koran. A man who can write such a koran, a man who can break with the intellectual tradition of mankind because he lives in the faith that a new truth and a new world begin with him, must be in a peculiar pneumopathological state. Hooker, who was supremely conscious of tradition, had a fine sensitiveness for this twist of mind. In his cautiously subdued characterization of Calvin he opened with the sober statement: "His bringing up was in the study of civil law"; he then built up with some malice: "Divine knowledge he gathered, not by hearing or reading so much, as by teaching others"; and he concluded on the devastating sentence: "For, though thousands were debtors to him, as touching knowledge in that kind; yet he (was debtor) to none but only to God, the author of the most blessed fountain, the Book of Life, and of the admirable dexterity of wit."[2]

The work of Calvin was the first but not the last of its kind; moreover, the genus had a prehistory. In the early phases of Western Gnostic sectarianism, the place of a koran was taken by the works of Scotus Eriugena and Dionysius Areopagita; and in the Joachitic movement the works of Joachim of Flora played this role under the title of *Evangelium aeternum*. In later Western history, in the period of secularization, new korans were produced with every wave of the movement. In the eighteenth century, Diderot and D'Alembert claimed koranic function for the *Encyclopédie française* as the comprehensive presentation of all human knowledge worth preserving. Ac-

2. *Ibid.*, pp. 127 ff.

cording to their conception, nobody would have to use any work antedating the *Encyclopédie*, and all future sciences would assume the form of supplements to the great collection of knowledge.[3] In the nineteenth century, Auguste Comte created his own work as the koran for the positivistic future of mankind but generously supplemented it by his list of the one hundred great books—an idea which still has retained its appeal. In the Communist movement, finally, the works of Karl Marx have become the koran of the faithful, supplemented by the patristic literature of Leninism-Stalinism.

The second device for preventing embarrassing criticism is a necessary supplement to the first one. The Gnostic koran is the codification of truth and as such the spiritual and intellectual nourishment of the faithful. From contemporary experience with totalitarian movements it is well known that the device is fairly foolproof because it can reckon with the voluntary censorship of the adherents; the faithful member of a movement will not touch literature that is apt to argue against, or show disrespect for, his cherished beliefs. Nevertheless, the number of faithful may remain small, and expansion and political success will be seriously hampered, if the truth of the Gnostic movement is permanently exposed to effective criticism from various quarters. This handicap can be reduced, and practically eliminated, by putting a taboo on the instruments of critique; a person who uses the tabooed instruments will be socially boycotted and, if possible, exposed to political defamation. The taboo on the instruments of critique was used, indeed, with superb effectiveness by the Gnostic movements wherever they reached a measure of political success. Concretely, in the wake of the Reformation, the taboo had to fall on classic philosophy and scholastic theology; and, since under these two heads came the major and certainly the de-

3. D'Alembert, *Discours préliminaire de l'Encyclopédie*, ed. F. Picavet (Paris, 1894), pp. 139–40.

cisive part of Western intellectual culture, this culture was ruined to the extent to which the taboo became effective. In fact, the destruction went so deep that Western society has never completely recovered from the blow. An incident from Hooker's life will illustrate the situation. The anonymous *Christian Letter* of 1599, addressed to Hooker, complained bitterly: "In all your books, although we finde manie trueths and fine points bravely handled, yet in all your discourse, for the most parte, Aristotle the patriarche of philosophers (with divers other humane writers) and the ingenuous schoolemen, almost in all points have some finger: reason is highlie sett up against Holy Scripture, and reading against preaching."[4] Such complaints about violations of the taboo were not innocuous expressions of opinion. In 1585, in the affair with Travers, Hooker had been the target of similar charges; and they closed on the denunciatory tone that such "absurdities . . . have not been heard in public places within this land since Queen Mary's day." In his answer to the Archbishop of Canterbury, Hooker very apologetically had to express his hope that he "committed no unlawful thing" when indulging in some theoretical distinctions and excursions in his sermons.[5]

Since gnosticism lives by the theoretical fallacies that were discussed in the preceding lecture, the taboo on theory in the classic sense is the ineluctable condition of its social expansion and survival. This has a serious consequence with regard to the possibility of public debate in societies where Gnostic movements have achieved social influence sufficient to control the means of communication, educational institutions, etc. To the degree to which such control is effective, theoretical debate concerning issues which involve the truth of human existence is impossible in public because the use of theoretical argument is prohibited. However well the constitutional freedoms of speech and press may be protected, however well theo-

4. Hooker, *op. cit.*, p. 373.　　　5. *Ibid.*, III, 585 ff.

retical debate may flourish in small circles, and however well it may be carried on in the practically private publications of a handful of scholars, debate in the politically relevant public sphere will be in substance the game with loaded dice which it has become in contemporary progressive societies—to say nothing of the quality of debate in totalitarian empires. Theoretical debate can be protected by constitutional guaranties, but it can be established only by the willingness to use and accept theoretical argument. When this willingness does not exist, a society cannot rely for its functioning on argument and persuasion where the truth of human existence is involved; other means will have to be considered.

This was the position of Hooker. Debate with his Puritan opponents was impossible because they would not accept argument. The ideas which he entertained in this predicament may be gathered from the notes jotted down shortly before his death on a copy of the previously quoted *Christian Letter*. Among the quotations from various authorities, there is a passage from Averroës:

Discourse (*sermo*) about the knowledge which God in His glory has of Himself and the world is prohibited. And even more so is it prohibited to put it in writing. For, the understanding of the vulgar does not reach such profundities; and when it becomes the subject of their discussions, the divinity will be destroyed with them. Hence, discussion of this knowledge is prohibited to them; and it is sufficient for their felicity if they understand what they can perceive by their intelligence. The law (that is: the *Koran*), whose primary intention it was to teach the vulgar, did not fail in intelligible communication about this subject because it is inaccessible to man; but we do not possess the human instruments that could assimilate God for intelligible communication about Him. As it is said: "His left hand founded the earth, but His right hand measured the Heaven." Hence, this question is reserved for the sage whom God dedicated to truth.[6]

6. For the Latin text of the passage see *ibid.*, I, cxix.

In this passage Averroës expressed the solution which the problem of theoretical debate had found in Islamic civilization. The nucleus of truth is the experience of transcendence in the anthropological and soteriological sense; its theoretical explication is communicable only among the "sage." The "vulgar" have to accept, in a simple fundamentalism, the truth as it is symbolized in Scripture; they must refrain from theoretization, for which experientially and intellectually they are unfit, because they only would destroy God. Considering the "murder of God" that was committed in Western society when the progressivist "vulgar" got their fingers on the meaning of human existence in society and history, one must admit that Averroës had a point.

The structure of a civilization, however, is not at the disposition of its individual members. The Islamic solution of confining philosophical debate to esoteric circles of whose existence the people at large was hardly aware could not be transferred to Hooker's situation. Western history had taken a different course, and the debate of the "vulgar" was well under way. Hence, Hooker had to contemplate the second possibility that a debate, which could not end with agreement through persuasion, would have to be closed by governmental authority. His Puritan opponents were not partners in a theoretical debate; they were Gnostic revolutionaries, engaged in a struggle for existential representation that would have resulted in the overthrow of the English social order, the control of the universities by Puritans, and the replacement of common law by scriptural law. Hence his consideration of this second solution was well in order. Hooker perfectly understood, what today is so little understood, that Gnostic propaganda is political action and not perhaps a search of truth in the theoretical sense. With his unerring sensitiveness he even diagnosed the nihilistic component of gnosticism in the Puritan belief that their discipline, being "the absolute command of Almighty God, it must be received although the world by receiving it should be clean turned upside down; herein lieth the greatest danger of all."[7] In the political culture of his time it was still clear beyond a doubt that the government, not the subjects, represents the order of a society. "As though when public consent of the whole hath established anything, every man's judgment being thereunto compared were not private, howsoever his calling be to some public charge. So that of peace and quietness there is not any way possible, unless the probable voice of every entire society or body politic overrule all private of like nature in the same body."[8] This means concretely that a government has the duty to preserve the order as well as the truth which it represents; when a Gnostic leader appears and proclaims that God or progress, race or dialectic, has ordained him to become the existential ruler, a government is not supposed to betray its trust and to abdicate. And this rule suffers no exception for governments which operate under a democratic constitution and a bill of rights. Justice Jackson in his dissent in the Terminiello case formulated the point: the Bill of Rights is not a suicide pact. A democratic government is not supposed to become an accomplice in its own overthrow by letting Gnostic movements grow prodigiously in the shelter of a muddy interpretation of civil rights; and if through inadvertence such a movement has grown to the danger point of capturing existential representation by the famous "legality" of popular elections, a democratic government is not supposed to bow to the "will of the people" but to put down the danger by force and, if necessary, to break the letter of the constitution in order to save its spirit.

4

Thus far Hooker—and now the other side must be heard. The first point to be considered will be the peculiar experience

7. *Ibid.*, p. 182.   8. *Ibid.*, p. 171.

of the Gnostic revolutionaries. Against the usual treatment of Puritanism as a Christian movement must be held the fact that there is no passage in the New Testament from which advice for revolutionary political action could be extracted; and even the Revelation of St. John, while burning with eschatological expectation of the realm that will deliver the saints from the oppression of this world, does not put the establishment of the realm into the hands of a Puritan army. The Gnostic revolutionary, however, interprets the coming of the realm as an event that requires his military co-operation. In chapter 20 of Revelation an angel comes down from heaven and throws Satan into the bottomless pit for a thousand years; in the Puritan Revolution the Gnostics arrogate this angelic function to themselves. A few passages from a pamphlet of 1641, entitled *A Glimpse of Sion's Glory*, will convey this peculiar mood of the Gnostic revolution.

The author of the pamphlet is animated by eschatological expectations.[9] The fall of Babylon is at hand; the new Jerusalem will come soon. "Babylon's falling is Sion's raising. Babylon's destruction is Jerusalem's salvation." While God is the ultimate cause of the imminent happy change, men should indulge in some meritorious action, too, in order to hasten the coming. "Blessed is he that dasheth the brats of Babylon against the stones. Blessed is he that hath any hand in pulling down Babylon." And who are the men who will hasten the coming of Zion by dashing the brats of Babylon against the stone? They are "the common people." "God intends to make use of the common people in the great work of proclaiming the kingdom of his Son." The common people have a privileged status in advancing the Kingdom of Christ. For the voice of Christ "comes first from the multitude, the common people. The voice is heard from them first, before it is heard

9. *A Glimpse of Sion's Glory* (1641), attributed to Hanserd Knollys, in *Puritanism and Liberty*, ed. A. S. P. Woodhouse (London, 1938), pp. 233–41.

from any others. God uses the common people and the multitude to proclaim that the Lord God Omnipotent reigneth." Christ did not come to the upper classes; he came to the poor. The noble, the wise, and the rich, and especially the prelacy, are possessed by the spirit of Antichrist; and, hence, the voice of Christ "is like to begin from those that are the multitude, that are so contemptible," from "the vulgar multitude." In the past "the people of God have been, and are, a despised people." The Saints are called factious, schismatics and Puritans, seditious and disturbers of the state. This stigma, however, shall be taken from them; and the rulers will become convinced in their hearts that "the inhabitants of Jerusalem, that is, the Saints of God gathered in a church, are the best commonwealth's men." And this conviction of the rulers will be fortified by drastic changes in social relations. The author quotes Isa. 49: 23: "Kings shall be thy nursing fathers, and queens thy nursing mothers; they shall bow down to thee, and lick up the dust of thy feet." The Saints, on the other hand, will be glorified in the new realm; they "shall be all clothed in white linen, which is the righteousness of the Saints."

Besides the sartorial reform for the Saints and the dust-licking for the rulers, there will be incisive changes in the structure of legal and economic institutions. With regard to legal institutions, the beauty and glory of the realm will quite probably make legal compulsion unnecessary. "It is questionable whether there shall be need of ordinances, at least in that way that now there is. . . . The presence of Christ shall be there and supply all kind of ordinances." With regard to economic conditions there shall be abundance and prosperity. The whole world is purchased by Christ for the Saints; and it will be delivered. "All is yours, says the Apostle, the whole world"; and most candidly the author supplies the motive for his conviction: "You see that the Saints have little now in this world; now they are the poorest and meanest of all; but then . . . the world shall be theirs. . . . Not only heaven shall be your kingdom, but this world bodily."

All this has nothing to do with Christianity. The scriptural camouflage cannot veil the drawing of God into man. The Saint is a Gnostic who will not leave the transfiguration of the world to the grace of God beyond history but will do the work of God himself, right here and now, in history. To be sure, the author of the pamphlet knows that not ordinary human powers will establish the realm but that human efforts will be subsidiary to the action of God. The Omnipotent God will come to the aid of the Saints and "shall do these things, by that power, whereby he is able to subdue all things unto himself. Mountains shall be made plain, and he shall come skipping over mountains and over difficulties. Nothing shall hinder him." But in this God who comes skipping over the mountains we recognize the dialectics of history that comes skipping over thesis and antithesis, until it lands its believers in the plain of the Communist synthesis.

The second point to be considered will be the program of the revolutionaries for the organization of society after the old world has been made new by their efforts. As a rule, Gnostics are not very explicit on this point. The new, transfigured world is supposed to be free of the evils of the old world; and the description will, therefore, ordinarily indulge in negations of the present grievances. The "glimpse" of Zion's glory is a category of Gnostic description rather than the title of a random pamphlet. The "glimpse" will typically reveal a state of prosperity and abundance, a minimum of work, and the abolition of governmental compulsion; and as an entertainment of rather common appeal there may be thrown in some maltreatment of members of the former upper class. Beyond such glimpses the description usually peters out; and the better thinkers among Gnostic revolutionaries, as, for instance, Marx and Engels, justify their reticence with the argument that one cannot say much about institutions of a transfigured society because we have no present experience of social relations under the condition of a transfigured nature of man. Fortunately, there is extant a Puritan document concerning the organization of the new world, in the form of the *Queries* directed by a group of Fifth Monarchy men to Lord Fairfax.[10]

At the time of the *Queries*, in 1649, the revolution was well under way; it had reached a stage corresponding to the stage of the Russian Revolution at which Lenin wrote about the "next tasks." In a similar manner one of the queries is phrased: "What then is the present interest of the Saints and people of God?" The reply advises that the Saints should associate in church societies and corporations according to the Congregational way; when enough such congregations have grown, they should combine into general assemblies or church parliaments according to the Presbyterian way; "and then shall God give them authority and rule over the nations and kingdoms of the world." Since this will be a spiritual kingdom, it cannot be established "by human power and authority." The Spirit itself will call and gather a people "and form them into several less families, churches and corporations"; and only when these spiritual nucleuses have sufficiently multiplied shall they "rule the world" through assemblies "of such officers of Christ, and representatives of the churches, as they shall choose and delegate." It all sounds comparatively harmless and harmonious; the worst that can happen will be some disillusionment when the Spirit takes its time in animating the new world.

As a matter of fact the affair is not quite so harmless. The Saints present their *Queries* to the Lord General of the Army and to the General Council of War. Under these conditions the formula that God will give the Saints "authority and rule over the nations and kingdoms of the world" sounds a dis-

10. *Certain Queries Presented by Many Christian People* (1649), pp. 241–47.

turbing note. One may ask: Who are these nations and kingdoms of the world over whom the Saints will rule? Are they
the nations and kingdoms of the old world? But in that case
we would, not yet be in the new world. And when we are in
the new world—over whom could the Saints rule except themselves? Or will there be some miscreant old-world nations left
whom the Saints can bully at their ease in order to add flavor
to their new ruling position? In brief: the shape of things to
come looks very much like what later Gnostics call the dictatorship of the proletariat.

The suspicion is confirmed by further details. The *Queries*
distinguish between "officers of Christ" and "Christian
magistrates." The rule of the spirit will put down all worldly
rule, including the rule of the Christian magistrates of England. The distinction is the best evidence that in revolutions
of the Puritan variety, indeed, two types of truth are strug-
gling for existential representation. The *Queries* accord the
name of Christianity to both types of truth, but the types are
so radically different that they represent the worlds of darkness and light, respectively. The Puritan victory may preserve
the structure of the world, including the parliamentary institutions of England, but the animating spirit will have radically changed. And this radical change will express itself politically in the radical change of the ruling personnel. The pe-
titioners ask persuasively: "Consider whether it be not a far
greater honour for parliaments, magistrates, etc., to rule as
Christ's officers and the churches' representatives than as officers of a worldly kingdom and representatives of a mere natural and worldly people?" It is not enough to be a Christian
representative of the English people in Parliament, for the
people as such belong in the natural order of the old world;
the member of Parliament must represent the Saints and the
communities of the new kingdom which are informed by the
Spirit itself. Hence, the old political ruling group must be

eliminated for "what right or claim have mere natural and worldly men to rule and government, that want a sanctified claim to the least outward blessings?" And even more pointedly: "How can the kingdom be the Saints' when the ungodly are electors, and elected to govern?" The attitude is uncompromising. If we expect new heavens and a new earth, "how then can it be lawful to patch up the old worldly government?" The only righteous course will be the one that results in "suppressing the enemies of godliness for ever."

No elaborate interpretation is necessary. A few modernizations of language are sufficient to bring out the meaning of these suggestions. The historical order of the people is broken by the rise of a movement which does not belong to "this world." Social evils cannot be reformed by legislation; defects of governmental machinery cannot be repaired by changes in the constitution; differences of opinion cannot be settled by compromise. "This world" is darkness that must give way to the new light. Hence, coalition governments are impossible. The political figures of the old order cannot be re-elected in the new world; and the men who are not members of the movement will be deprived of their right to vote in the new order. All these changes will arrive substantially through the "Spirit" or, as Gnostics would say today, through the dialectics of history; but in political procedure the saintly comrades will take a hand, and the hand will be well armed. If the personnel of the old order should not disappear with a smile, the enemies of godliness will be suppressed or, in contemporary language, will be purged. In the *Queries* the realization of the new world has reached the stage at which, in the Russian Revolution, Lenin wrote his reflections under the coquettish title, "Will the Bolsheviks Retain State Power?" They will, indeed; and nobody will share it with them.

The new kingdom will be universal in substance as well as universal in its claim to dominion; it will extend "to all persons and things universally." The revolution of the Gnostics has for its aim the monopoly of existential representation. The Saints can foresee that the universalism of their claim will not be accepted without a struggle by the world of darkness but that it will produce an equally universal alliance of the world against them. The Saints, therefore, will have to combine "against the Antichristian powers of the world"; and the Antichristian powers in their turn will "combine against them universally." The two worlds which are supposed to follow each other chronologically will, thus, become in historical reality two universal armed camps engaged in a death struggle against each other. From the Gnostic mysticism of the two worlds emerges the pattern of the universal wars that has come to dominate the twentieth century. The universalism of the Gnostic revolutionary produces the universal alliance against him. The real danger of contemporary wars does not lie in the technologically determined global extent of the theater of war; their true fatality stems from their character as Gnostic wars, that is, of wars between worlds that are bent on mutual destruction.

The selection of materials which are meant to illustrate nature and direction of the Gnostic revolution may seem unfair. A critic might object that Puritanism as a whole cannot be identified with its left wing. Such criticism would be justified if it had been the intention to give a historical account of Puritanism. The present analysis, however, is concerned with the structure of Gnostic experiences and ideas; and this structure is also to be found where the consequences are toned down to the respectability of Calvin's *Institutes* or of Presbyterian covenantism. The amplitude from right to left within every wave of the movement, the struggle between the two wings on occasion of the acute outbreaks in the several national areas, as well as the temporary stabilizations of a viable order, are phenomena within the Gnostic revolution that will receive further attention in the last of these lectures. These phenomena, the dynamics of the revolution, however, do not affect its nature; and the nature can, indeed, be studied best in its radical expressions where it is not obscured by compromises with the exigencies of political success. Moreover, this is not a mere matter of convenience but a methodological necessity. The Gnostic revolution has for its purpose a change in the nature of man and the establishment of a transfigured society. Since this program cannot be carried out in historical reality, Gnostic revolutionaries must inevitably institutionalize their partial or total success in the existential struggle by a compromise with reality; and whatever emerges from this compromise—it will not be the transfigured world envisaged by Gnostic symbolism. If, therefore, the theorist would study the Gnostic revolution at the level of its temporary stabilizations, of its political tactics, or of the moderate programs which already envisage the compromise, the nature of gnosticism, the driving force of Western revolution, could never come into view. The compromise would be taken for the essence, and the essential unity of the variegated Gnostic phenomena would disappear.

5

The English revolution made it clear that the struggle of Gnostic revolutionaries for existential representation could destroy the public order of a great nation—if such proof was needed after the eight civil wars in France and the Thirty Years' War in Germany. The problem of public order was overdue for theoretical restatement, and in Thomas Hobbes this task found a thinker who was equal to it. The new theory of representation which Hobbes developed in the *Leviathan*, to be sure, purchased its impressive consistency at the price of a simplification which itself belongs in the class of Gnostic misdeeds; but, when a fierce and relentless thinker simplifies,

he will nevertheless bring a new clarity to the issue. The simplification can be repaired, while the new clarity will be a
permanent gain.

The Hobbesian theory of representation cuts straight to the
core of the predicament. On the one hand, there is a political
society that wants to maintain its established order in historical existence; on the other hand, there are private individuals within the society who want to change the public order,
if necessary by force, in the name of a new truth. Hobbes
solved the conflict by deciding that there was no public truth
except the law of peace and concord in a society; any opinion
or doctrine conducive to discord was thereby proved untrue.[11]
In order to support his decision, Hobbes used the following
argument:

(1) There is conscious to man a dictate of reason which disposes
him to peace and obedience under a civil order. Reason makes him,
first, understand that he can live out his natural life in pursuit of his
worldly happiness only under the condition that he lives in peace
with his fellow-men; and it makes him, second, understand that he
can live in peace, without distrust of the other man's intentions,
only under the condition that every man's passions are curbed to
mutual forbearance by the overwhelming force of a civil government.[12]

(2) This dictate of reason, however, would be no more than a
theorem without obligatory force unless it were understood as the
hearing of the word of God, as His command promulgated in the
soul of man; only in so far as the dictate of reason is believed to be
a divine command is it a law of nature.[13]

(3) This law of nature, finally, is not a law actually governing
human existence before the men, in whom it lives as a disposition
toward peace, have followed its precept by combining in a civil
society under a public representative, the sovereign. Only when they

11. Thomas Hobbes, *Leviathan*, ed. Michael Oakeshott (Blackstone ed.; Oxford,
s.a.), chap. xviii, p. 116.
12. *Ibid.*, chap. xiv.
13. *Ibid.*, chap. xv, pp. 104 ff.; chap. xxxi, p. 233.

have covenanted to submit to a common sovereign, has the law of nature actually become the law of a society in historical existence.[14] "The law of nature, and the civil law, therefore, contain each other, and are of equal extent."[15]

Existential and transcendental representation, thus, meet in the articulation of a society into ordered existence. By combining into a political society under a representative, the covenanting members actualize the divine order of being in the human sphere.[16]

Into this somewhat empty vessel of a political society, now, Hobbes pours the Western-Christian civilizational content by letting it pass through the bottleneck of sanction by the sovereign representative. The society may well be a Christian commonwealth because the Word of God revealed in Scripture is not at variance with natural law.[17] Nevertheless, the canon of Scripture to be received,[18] the doctrinal and ritual interpretations put on it,[19] as well as the form of clerical organization,[20] will derive their authority not from revelation but from the enactment by the sovereign as the law of the land. There will be no freedom of debate concerning the truth of human existence in society; public expression of opinion and doctrine must be under regulation and permanent supervision of the government. "For the actions of men proceed from their opinions; and in the well-governing of opinions, consisteth the well-governing of men's actions, in order to their peace, and concord." Hence, the sovereign has to decide who will be allowed to speak in public to an audience, on what subject and in what tendency; there will be necessary, furthermore, a preventive censorship of books.[21] For the rest, there will be freedom for the peaceable, civilizational pursuits of the citizens,

---

14. *Ibid.*, chap. xv, p. 94.
15. *Ibid.*, chap. xxvi, p. 174.
16. *Ibid.*, chap. xxxi, p. 233.
17. *Ibid.*, chap. xxxii, p. 242.

18. *Ibid.*, chap. xxxiii, pp. 246 ff.
19. *Ibid.*, pp. 254 ff.
20. *Ibid.*, chap. xlii, pp. 355–56.
21. *Ibid.*, chap. xviii, pp. 116 ff.

since this is the purpose for which men combine in a civil society.[22]

In judging the Hobbesian theory of representation, one must avoid the ready pitfalls of current political jargon. Nothing can be gained from weighing the theory on the scales of liberty and authority; nothing from classifying Hobbes as an absolutist or Fascist. A critical interpretation must follow the theoretical intentions indicated by Hobbes himself in his work. These intentions can be gathered from the following passage:

For it is evident to the meanest capacity, that men's actions are derived from their opinions they have of the good or evil, which from those actions redound unto themselves; and consequently, men that are once possessed of an opinion, that their obedience to the sovereign power will be more hurtful to them than their disobedience, will disobey the laws, and thereby overthrow the commonwealth, and introduce confusion and civil war; for the avoiding whereof all civil government was ordained. And therefore in all commonwealths of the heathen, the sovereigns have had the name of pastors of the people, because there was no subject that could lawfully teach the people, but by their permission and authority.

And it cannot be the purpose of Christianity, Hobbes continues, to deprive the sovereigns "of the power necessary for the conservation of peace amongst their subjects, and for their defence against foreign enemies."[23]

From the passage emerges Hobbes's intention of establishing Christianity (understood as identical in substance with the law of nature) as an English *theologia civilis* in the Varronic sense. At the first hearing such an intention may sound self-contradictory. How can the Christian *theologia supranaturalis* be established as a *theologia civilis*? In making this curious attempt, Hobbes brought into the open a problem that was left in suspense in our own earlier analysis of the *genera*

22. *Ibid.*, chap. xxi, pp. 138 ff.   23. *Ibid.*, chap. xlii, p. 355.

theologiae and their conflict in the Roman Empire. You will remember that St. Ambrose and St. Augustine were oddly insensitive to the fact that a Christian on the throne would, under their guidance, treat pagans in the same manner in which pagan emperors had formerly treated Christians. They understood Christianity as a truth of the soul superior to polytheism but did not recognize that the Roman gods symbolized the truth of Roman society; that with the cult a culture was destroyed, as Celsus had discerned; that an existential victory of Christianity was not a conversion of individual human beings to a higher truth but the forceful imposition of a new *theologia civilis* on a society. In the case of Hobbes the situation is reversed. When he treats Christianity under the aspect of its substantial identity with the dictate of reason and derives its authority from governmental sanction, he shows himself as oddly insensitive to its meaning as a truth of the soul as were the Patres to the meaning of the Roman gods as a truth of society. In order to reach the root of these oddities, it will be necessary to reconsider the epochal event of the opening of the soul and to add a theoretical distinction.

The opening of the soul was an epochal event in the history of mankind because, with the differentiation of the soul as the sensorium of transcendence, the critical, theoretical standards for the interpretation of human existence in society, as well as the source of their authority, came into view. When the soul opened toward transcendent reality, it found a source of order superior in rank to the established order of society as well as a truth in critical opposition to the truth at which society had arrived through the symbolism of its self-interpretation. Moreover, the idea of a universal God as the measure of the open soul had as its logical correlate the idea of a universal community of mankind, beyond civil society, through the participation of all men in the common measure, be it understood as the Aristotelian *nous*, the Stoic or the Christian *logos*. The impact of such discoveries might well obscure the fact that the new clarity about the structure of reality had not changed this structure itself. The opening of the soul, indeed, marked an epoch through its advancement from compactness to differentiation of experience, from dimness to clarity of insight; but the tension between a truth of society and a truth of the soul had existed before this epoch, and the new understanding of transcendence could sharpen the consciousness of the tension but not remove it from the constitution of being. The idea of a universal God, for instance, achieved its specific purity through the mystic philosophers, but its existence, imbedded in a compact cosmological myth, is attested by Egyptian inscriptions for about 3000 B.C.; and since, even at this early date, the idea appeared in the course of a polemical, critical speculation on hierarchy and function of gods, there must have existed the tension between a truth as understood by the speculating thinker and the truth of the received myth.[24] The Stoic understanding of the cosmopolis to which men belong by virtue of their participation in the Logos, on the other hand, did not abolish the existence of man in finite historical societies. Hence, we must distinguish between the opening of the soul as an epoch in experiential differentiation and the structure of reality which remains unchanged.

From the distinction it follows for the present problem that the tension between a differentiated truth of the soul and the truth of society cannot be eliminated from historical reality by throwing out the one or the other. Human existence in natural societies remains what it was before its orientation toward a destiny beyond nature. Faith is the anticipation of a supernatural perfection of man; it is not this perfection itself. The realm of God is not of this world; and the representative

24. William F. Albright, *From the Stone Age to Christianity: Monotheism and the Historical Process* (Baltimore, 1946), pp. 132 ff.; Hermann Junker, *Pyramidenzeit: Das Wesen der altägyptischen Religion* (Zurich, 1949), pp. 18 ff.

of the *civitas Dei* in history, the church, is not a substitute for civil society. The result of the epochal differentiation is not the replacement of the closed society by an open society—if we may use the Bergsonian terms—but a complication of symbolism which corresponds to the differentiation of experiences. Both types of truth will from now on exist together; and the tension between the two, in various degrees of consciousness, will be a permanent structure of civilization. This insight had been gained already by Plato; in his work it is reflected in the evolution from the *Republic* to the *Laws*. In the *Republic* he constructed a polis that would incarnate the truth of the soul under the immediate rule of mystic philosophers; it was an attempt to dissolve the tension by making the order of the soul the order of society. In the *Laws* he removed the truth of the soul into the distance of its revelation in the *Republic;* the polis of the *Laws* relied on institutions that mirrored the order of the cosmos, while the truth of the soul was mediated by administrators who received it as dogma. Plato himself, the potential philosopher-king of the *Republic*, became the Athenian Stranger of the *Laws* who assisted in devising institutions that embodied as much of the spirit as was compatible with the continued natural existence of society.

The Christian Patres did not display the perspicacity of Plato when the same problem was forced upon them by historical circumstance. Apparently they did not understand that Christianity could supersede polytheism but not abolish the need of a civil theology. When the truth of the soul had prevailed, the vacuum was left that Plato had tried to fill with his construction of the polis as a cosmic analogue. The filling of this vacuum became a major problem wherever Christianity dissolved the pre-Christian truth of the closed society as a living force; wherever, as a consequence, the church achieved existential representation by the side of the civil ruler and now had to provide transcendental legitimation for the order of society, in addition to its representation of the supranatural destiny of man. The one great solution was Byzantine caesaropapism, with its tendency toward transforming the church into a civil institution. Against this tendency, at the end of the fifth century, Gelasius wrote his letters and tracts which formulated the other great solution, that of the two balancing powers. This balance functioned in the West as long as the work of civilizational expansion and consolidation provided parallel interests for ecclesiastic and civil organizations. But the tension between the two types of truth became noticeable as soon as a certain degree of civilizational saturation was reached. When the church, in the wake of the Cluniac reform, reasserted its spiritual substance and tried to disengage itself from its civil entanglements, the investiture struggle was the consequence. On the other hand, when the Gnostic sectarian movements gained momentum in the twelfth century, the church co-operated, through the Inquisition, with the civil power in the persecution of heretics; it leaned strongly toward its function as the agent of the *theologia civilis* and thereby became untrue to its essence as the representative of the *civitas Dei* in history. The tension, finally, reached the breaking point when a plurality of schismatic churches and Gnostic movements entered into violent competition for existential representation. The vacuum now became manifest in the religious civil wars.

Hobbes saw that public order was impossible without a civil theology beyond debate; it is the great and permanent achievement of the *Leviathan* to have clarified this point. Less fortunate was his hand when he tried to fill the vacuum by establishing Christianity as the English civil theology. He could entertain this idea because he assumed Christianity, if properly interpreted, to be identical with the truth of society which he had developed in the first two parts of the *Leviathan*. He denied the existence of a tension between the truth of the soul and the truth of society; the content of Scripture, in his opinion, coincided in substance with the truth of Hobbes. On the basis of this assumption, he could indulge in the idea of solving a crisis of world-historical proportions by tendering his expert advice to any sovereign who was willing to take it. "I recover some hope," he said, "that one time or other, this writing of mine may fall into the hands of a sovereign, who will consider it himself, (for it is short, and I think clear), without the help of any interested, or envious interpreter; and by the exercise of entire sovereignty, in protecting the public teaching of it, convert this truth of speculation, into the utility of practice."[25] He saw himself in the role of a Plato, in quest of a king who would adopt the new truth and indoctrinate the people with it. The education of the people was an essential part of his program. Hobbes did not rely on governmental force for suppressing religious movements; he knew that public order was genuine only if the people accepted it freely and that free acceptance was possible only if the people understood obedience to the public representative as their duty under eternal law. If the people were ignorant of this law, they would consider punishment for rebellion an "act of hostility; which when they think they have strength enough, they will endeavour by acts of hostility, to avoid." He, therefore, declared it the duty of the sovereign to repair the ignorance of the people by appropriate information. If that were done, there might be hope that his principles would "make their constitution, excepting by external violence, everlasting."[26] With this idea, however, of abolishing the tensions of history by the spreading of a new truth, Hobbes reveals his own Gnostic intentions; the attempt at freezing history into an everlasting constitution is an instance of the general class of Gnostic

25. Hobbes, *op. cit.*, chap. xxxi, p. 241.
26. *Ibid.*, chap. xxx, pp. 220 ff.

attempts at freezing history into an everlasting final realm on this earth.

The idea of solving the troubles of history through the invention of the everlasting constitution made sense only under the condition that the source of these troubles, that is, the truth of the soul, would cease to agitate man. Hobbes, indeed, simplified the structure of politics by throwing out anthropological and soteriological truth. This is an understandable desire in a man who wants his peace; things, to be sure, would be so much simpler without philosophy and Christianity. But how can one dispose of them without abolishing the experiences of transcendence which belong to the nature of man? Hobbes was quite able to solve this problem, too; he improved on the man of God's creation by creating a man without such experiences. At this point, however, we are entering the higher regions of the Gnostic dream world. This further Hobbesian enterprise must be placed in the larger context of the Western crisis; and that will be a task for the last of these lectures.

VI

THE END OF MODERNITY

�֢

1

HOBBES had discerned the lack of a *theologia civilis* as the source of difficulties that plagued the state of England in the Puritan crisis. The various groups engaged in the civil war were so heaven-bent on having the public order represent the right variety of transcendent truth that the existential order of society was in danger of floundering in the melee. It certainly was an occasion to rediscover the discovery of Plato that a society must exist as an ordered cosmion, as a representative of cosmic order, before it can indulge in the luxury of also representing a truth of the soul. To represent the truth of the soul in the Christian sense is the function of the church, not of civil society. If a plurality of churches and sects starts fighting for control of the public order, and none of them is strong enough to gain an unequivocal victory, the logical result can only be that, by the existential authority of the public representative, the whole lot will be relegated to the position of private associations within the society. This problem of existence was touched on several occasions in these lectures; it now requires a summary elucidation before the Hobbesian idea of man can be presented and evaluated. The analysis will suitably start from the points that have already been secured.

Christianity had left in its wake the vacuum of a de-divinized natural sphere of political existence. In the concrete situation of the late Roman Empire and the early Western political foundations, this vacuum did not become a major source of troubles as long as the myth of the empire was not seriously disturbed by the consolidation of national realms and as long as the church was the predominant civilizing factor in the evolution of Western society, so that Christianity in fact could function as a civil theology. As soon, however, as a certain point of civilizational saturation was reached, when centers of lay culture formed at the courts and in the cities, when competent lay personnel increased in royal administrations and city governments, it became abundantly clear that the problems of a society in historical existence were not exhausted by waiting for the end of the world. The rise of gnosticism at this critical juncture now appears in a new light as the incipient formation of a Western civil theology. The immanentization of the Christian eschaton made it possible to endow society in its natural existence with a meaning which Christianity denied to it. And the totalitarianism of our time must be understood as journey's end of the Gnostic search for a civil theology.

The Gnostic experiment in civil theology, however, was fraught with dangers, flowing from its hybrid character as a Christian derivative. The first of these dangers has been discussed already. It was the tendency of gnosticism not to supplement but to supplant the truth of the soul. Gnostic movements were not satisfied with filling the vacuum of civil theology; they tended to abolish Christianity. In the earlier phases of the movement the attack was still disguised as Christian "spiritualization" or "reform"; in the later phases, with the more radical immanentization of the eschaton, it became openly anti-Christian. As a consequence, wherever Gnostic movements spread they destroyed the truth of the open soul; a whole area of differentiated reality that had been gained by philosophy and Christianity was ruined. And again it is necessary to remember that the advance of gnosticism is not a return to paganism. In the pre-Christian civilizations the truth which differentiated with the opening of the soul was present in the form of compact experiences; in Gnostic civilizations the truth of the soul does not return to compactness but is repressed altogether. This repression of the authoritative source of order in the soul is the cause of the bleak atrocity of totalitarian governments in their dealings with individual human beings.

The peculiar, repressive result of the growth of gnosticism in Western society suggests the conception of a civilizational cycle of world-historic proportions. There emerge the contours of a giant cycle, transcending the cycles of the single civilizations. The acme of this cycle would be marked by the appearance of Christ; the pre-Christian high civilizations would form its ascending branch; modern, Gnostic civilization would form its descending branch. The pre-Christian high civilizations advanced from the compactness of experience to the differentiation of the soul as the sensorium of transcendence; and, in the Mediterranean civilizational area, this evolution culminated in the maximum of differentiation, through the revelation of the Logos in history. In so far as the pre-Christian civilizations advance toward this maximum of the advent, their dynamics may be called "adventitious." Modern Gnostic civilization reverses the tendency toward differentiation; and, in so far as it recedes from the maximum, its dynamics may be called "recessive." While Western society has its own cycle of growth, flowering, and decline, it must be considered—because of the growth of gnosticism in its course—as the declining branch of the larger advent-recession cycle.

These reflections open a perspective on the future dynamics of civilization. Modern gnosticism has by far not spent its drive. On the contrary, in the variant of Marxism it is expanding its area of influence prodigiously in Asia, while other variants of gnosticism, such as progressivism, positivism, and scientism, are penetrating into other areas under the title of "Westernization" and development of backward countries.

And one may say that in Western society itself the drive is not spent but that our own "Westernization" is still on the increase. In the face of this world-wide expansion it is necessary to state the obvious: that human nature does not change. The closure of the soul in modern gnosticism can repress the truth of the soul, as well as the experiences which manifest themselves in philosophy and Christianity, but it cannot remove the soul and its transcendence from the structure of reality. Hence the question imposes itself: How long can such a repression last? And what will happen when prolonged and severe repression will lead to an explosion? It is legitimate to ask such questions concerning the dynamics of the future because they spring from a methodically correct application of theory to an empirically observed component of contemporary civilization. It would not be legitimate, however, to indulge in speculations about the form which the explosion will assume, beyond the reasonable assumption that the reaction against gnosticism will be as world wide as its expansion. The number of complicating factors is so large that predictions seem futile. Even for our own Western society one can hardly do more than point to the fact that gnosticism, in spite of its noisy ascendancy, does by far not have the field for itself; that the classic and Christian tradition of Western society is rather alive; that the building-up of spiritual and intellectual resistance against gnosticism in all its variants is a notable factor in our society; that the reconstruction of a science of man and society is one of the remarkable events of the last half-century and, in retrospect from a future vantage point, will perhaps appear as the most important event in our time. Still less can be said, for obvious reasons, about the probable reaction of a living Christian tradition against gnosticism in the Soviet empire. And nothing at all about the manner in which Chinese, Hindu, Islamic, and primitive civilizations will react to a prolonged exposure to Gnostic devastation and repression. Only on one point at least a reasonable surmise is possible, that is, on the date of the explosion. The date in objective time, of course, is quite unpredictable; but gnosticism contains a self-defeating factor, and this factor makes it at least probable that the date is less distant than one would assume under the impression of Gnostic power of the moment. This self-defeating factor is the second danger of gnosticism as a civil theology.

2

The first danger was the destruction of the truth of the soul. The second danger is intimately connected with the first one. The truth of gnosticism is vitiated, as you will remember, by the fallacious immanentization of the Christian eschaton. This fallacy is not simply a theoretical mistake concerning the meaning of the eschaton, committed by this or that thinker, perhaps an affair of the schools. On the basis of this fallacy, Gnostic thinkers, leaders, and their followers interpret a concrete society and its order as an eschaton; and, in so far as they apply their fallacious construction to concrete social problems, they misrepresent the structure of immanent reality. The eschatological interpretation of history results in a false picture of reality; and errors with regard to the structure of reality have practical consequences when the false conception is made the basis of political action. Specifically, the Gnostic fallacy destroys the oldest wisdom of mankind concerning the rhythm of growth and decay which is the fate of all things under the sun. The Kohelet says:

> To every thing there is a season,
> And a time to every purpose under heaven:
> A time to be born and a time to die.

And then, reflecting on the finiteness of human knowledge, the Kohelet continues to say that the mind of man cannot fathom "the work that God maketh from the beginning to

the end."[1] What comes into being will have an end, and the
mystery of this stream of being is impenetrable. These are the
two great principles governing existence. The Gnostic speculation on the eidos of history, however, not only ignores these
principles but perverts them into their opposite. The idea of
the final realm assumes a society that will come into being but
have no end, and the mystery of the stream is solved through
the speculative knowledge of its goal. Gnosticism, thus, has
produced something like the counterprinciples to the principles of existence; and, in so far as these principles determine an
image of reality for the masses of the faithful, it has created a
dream world which itself is a social force of the first importance in motivating attitudes and actions of Gnostic
masses and their representatives.

The phenomenon of a dream world, based on definite principles, requires some explanation. It could hardly be possible as
a historical mass phenomenon unless it were rooted in a fundamental experiential drive. Gnosticism as a counterexistential
dream world can perhaps be made intelligible as the extreme
expression of an experience which is universally human, that
is, of a horror of existence and a desire to escape from it. Specifically, the problem can be stated in the following terms: A
society, when it exists, will interpret its order as part of the
transcendent order of being. This self-interpretation of society
as a mirror of cosmic order, however, is part of social reality
itself. The ordered society, together with its self-understanding, remains a wave in the stream of being; the Aeschylean
polis with its ordering Dike is an island in a sea of demonic
disorder, precariously maintaining itself in existence. Only the
order of an existing society is intelligible; its existence itself is
unintelligible. The successful articulation of a society is a fact
that has become possible under favorable circumstances; and
this fact may be annulled by unfavorable circumstances, as,

1. Eccles. 3:1–2 and 3:11.

for instance, by the appearance of a stronger, conquering power. The *fortuna secunda et adversa* is the smiling and terrible goddess who rules over this realm of existence. This hazard of existence without right or reason is a demonic horror; it is hard to bear even for the stronghearted; and it is hardly bearable for tender souls who cannot live without believing they deserve to live. It is a reasonable assumption, therefore, that in every society there is present, in varying degrees of intenseness, the inclination to extend the meaning of its order to the fact of its existence. Especially, when a society has a long and glorious history, its existence will be taken for granted as part of the order of things. It has become unimaginable that the society could simply cease to exist; and when a great symbolic blow falls, as, for instance, when Rome was conquered in 410, a groan went through the *orbis terrarum* that now the end of the world had come.

In every society, thus, is present an inclination to extend the meaning of order to the fact of existence, but in predominantly Gnostic societies this extension is erected into a principle of self-interpretation. This shift from a mood, from a lassitude to take existence for granted, to a principle determines a new pattern of conduct. In the first case, one can speak of an inclination to disregard the structure of reality, of relaxing into the sweetness of existence, of a decline of civic morality, of a blindness to obvious dangers, and a reluctance to meet them with all seriousness. It is the mood of late, disintegrating societies that no longer are willing to fight for their existence. In the second, the Gnostic case, the psychological situation is entirely different. In gnosticism the nonrecognition of reality is a matter of principle; in this case, one would have rather to speak of an inclination to remain aware of the hazard of existence in spite of the fact that it is not admitted as a problem in the Gnostic dream world; nor does the dream impair civic responsibility or the readiness to fight valiantly in case of an emergency. The attitude toward reality remains energetic and active, but neither reality nor action in reality can be brought into focus; the vision is blurred by the Gnostic dream. The result is a very complex pneumopathological state of mind, as it was adumbrated by Hooker's portrait of the Puritan.

The study of the phenomenon in its contemporary varieties, however, has become more difficult than it was at Hooker's time. In the sixteenth century the dream world and the real world were still held apart terminologically through the Christian symbolism of the two worlds. The disease, and its special variety, could be diagnosed easily because the patient himself was supremely conscious that the new world was not the world in which he lived in reality. With radical immanentization the dream world has blended into the real world terminologically; the obsession of replacing the world of reality by the transfigured dream world has become the obsession of the one world in which the dreamers adopt the vocabulary of reality, while changing its meaning, as if the dream were reality.

An example will best show the nature of the difficulty for the student. In classic and Christian ethics the first of the moral virtues is *sophia* or *prudentia*, because without adequate understanding of the structure of reality, including the *conditio humana*, moral action with rational co-ordination of means and ends is hardly possible. In the Gnostic dream world, on the other hand, nonrecognition of reality is the first principle. As a consequence, types of action which in the real world would be considered as morally insane because of the real effects which they have will be considered moral in the dream world because they intended an entirely different effect. The gap between intended and real effect will be imputed not to the Gnostic immorality of ignoring the structure of reality but to the immorality of some other person or society that does not behave as it should behave according to the dream conception of cause and effect. The interpretation of moral insanity as morality, and of the virtues of *sophia* and *prudentia* as immorality, is a confusion difficult to unravel. And the task is not facilitated by the readiness of the dreamers to stigmatize the attempt at critical clarification as an immoral enterprise. As a matter of fact, practically every great political thinker who recognized the structure of reality, from Machiavelli to the present, has been branded as an immoralist by Gnostic intellectuals—to say nothing of the parlor game, so much beloved among liberals, of panning Plato and Aristotle as Fascists. The theoretical difficulty, therefore, is aggravated by personal problems. And there can be no doubt that the continuous Gnostic barrage of vituperation against political science in the critical sense has seriously affected the quality of public debate on contemporary political issues.

The identification of dream and reality as a matter of principle has practical results which may appear strange but can hardly be considered surprising. The critical exploration of cause and effect in history is prohibited; and consequently the rational co-ordination of means and ends in politics is impossible. Gnostic societies and their leaders will recognize dangers to their existence when they develop, but such dangers will not be met by appropriate actions in the world of reality. They will rather be met by magic operations in the dream world, such as disapproval, moral condemnation, declarations of intention, resolutions, appeals to the opinion of mankind, branding of enemies as aggressors, outlawing of war, propaganda for world peace and world government, etc. The intellectual and moral corruption which expresses itself in the aggregate of such magic operations may pervade a society with the weird, ghostly atmosphere of a lunatic asylum, as we experience it in our time in the Western crisis.

A complete study of the manifestations of Gnostic insanity

in the practice of contemporary politics would go far beyond the framework of this lecture. The analysis must concentrate on the symptom that will best illustrate the self-defeating character of Gnostic politics, that is, the oddity of continuous warfare in a time when every political society, through its representatives, professes its ardent desire for peace. In an age when war is peace, and peace is war, a few definitions will be in order to assure the meaning of the terms. Peace shall mean a temporary order of social relations which adequately expresses a balance of existential forces. The balance may be disturbed by various causes, such as population increases in one area or decreases in another one, technological developments which favor areas rich in the necessary raw materials, changes of trade routes, etc. War shall mean the use of violence for the purpose of restoring a balanced order by either repressing the disturbing increase of existential force or by reordering social relations so that they will adequately express the new relative strength of existential forces. Politics shall mean the attempt to restore the balance of forces or to readjust the order, by various diplomatic means, or by building up discouraging counterforces short of war. These definitions should not be taken for the last word of wisdom in such formidable matters as war, peace, and politics but merely as a declaration of the rules that will govern the formulation of the present problem.

Gnostic politics is self-defeating in the sense that measures which are intended to establish peace increase the disturbances that will lead to war. The mechanics of this self-defeat has just been set forth in the description of magic operations in the dream world. If an incipient disturbance of the balance is not met by appropriate political action in the world of reality, if instead it is met with magic incantations, it may grow to such proportions that war becomes inevitable. The model case is the rise of the National Socialist movement to power, first in Germany, then on the continental scale, with the Gnostic

chorus wailing its moral indignation at such barbarian and reactionary doings in a progressive world—without however
raising a finger to repress the rising force by a minor political
effort in proper time. The prehistory of the second World War
raises the serious question whether the Gnostic dream has not
corroded Western society so deeply that rational politics has
become impossible, and war is the only instrument left for ad-
justing disturbances in the balance of existential forces.

The conduct of the war and its aftermath unfortunately are
apt to confirm this fear rather than to assuage it. If a war has a
purpose at all, it is the restoration of a balance of forces and
not the aggravation of disturbance; it is the reduction of the
unbalancing excess of force, not the destruction of force to the
point of creating a new unbalancing power vacuum. Instead
the Gnostic politicians have put the Soviet army on the Elbe,
surrendered China to the Communists, at the same time demil-
itarized Germany and Japan, and in addition demobilized our
own army. The facts are trite, and yet it is perhaps not sufficiently realized that never before in the history of mankind
has a world power used a victory deliberately for the purpose
of creating a power vacuum to its own disadvantage. And
again, as in previous contexts, it is necessary to warn that
phenomena of this magnitude cannot be explained by ignorance and stupidity. These policies were pursued as a matter of
principle, on the basis of Gnostic dream assumptions about
the nature of man, about a mysterious evolution of mankind
toward peace and world order, about the possibility of establishing an international order in the abstract without relation
to the structure of the field of existential forces, about armies
being the cause of war and not the forces and constellations
which build them and set them into motion, etc. The enumerated series of actions, as well as the dream assumptions on
which they are based, seem to show that the contact with reality is at least badly damaged and that the pathological sub-
stitution of the dream world is fairly effective.

Moreover, it should be noted that the unique phenomenon of a great power creating a power vacuum to its own disadvantage was accompanied by the equally unique phenomenon of military conclusion of a war without conclusion of peace treaties. This rather disturbing further phenomenon again cannot be explained by the baffling complexity of the problems that require settlement. It is again the dream obsession that makes it impossible for the representatives of Gnostic societies to formulate policies which take into account the structure of reality. There can be no peace, because the dream cannot be translated into reality and reality has not yet broken the dream. No one, of course, can predict what nightmares of violence it will take to break the dream, and still less so what Western society will look like *au bout de la nuit*.

Gnostic politics, thus, is self-defeating in so far as its disregard for the structure of reality leads to continuous warfare. This system of chain wars can end only in one of two ways. Either it will result in horrible physical destructions and concomitant revolutionary changes of social order beyond reasonable guesses; or, with the natural change of generations, it will lead to the abandoning of Gnostic dreaming before the worst has happened. In this sense should be understood the earlier suggestion that the end of the Gnostic dream is perhaps closer at hand than one ordinarily would assume.

3

This exposition of the dangers of gnosticism as a civil theology of Western society will probably have aroused some misgivings. The analysis did fully pertain only to the progressive and idealistic varieties which prevail in Western democracies; it would not equally well apply to the activist varieties which prevail in totalitarian empires. Whatever share of responsibility for the present plight may be laid on the doorsteps of progressivists and idealists, the most formidable source of imminent danger seems to be the activists. The intimate connec-

tion between the two dangers, therefore, requires clarification
—all the more so because the representatives of the two Gnostic varieties are antagonists in battle on the world scene. The
analysis of this further question can appropriately use as a
preface the pronouncements of a famous liberal intellectual on
the problem of communism:

Lenin was surely right when the end he sought for was to build
his heaven on earth and write the precepts of his faith into the inner
fabric of a universal humanity. He was surely right, too, when he
recognized that the prelude to peace is a war, and that it is futile to
suppose that the tradition of countless generations can be changed,
as it were, overnight.[2]

The power of any supernatural religion to build that tradition has
gone; the deposit of scientific inquiry since Descartes has been fatal
to its authority. It is therefore difficult to see upon what basis the
civilized tradition can be rebuilt save that upon which the idea of
the Russian Revolution is founded. It corresponds, its supernatural
basis apart, pretty exactly to the mental climate in which Christianity became the official religion of the West.[3]

It is, indeed, true in a sense to argue that the Russian principle
cuts deeper than the Christian since it seeks salvation for the masses
by fulfilment in this life, and, thereby, orders anew the actual world
we know.[4]

Few passages could be more revealing for the plight of the
liberal intellectual in our time. Philosophy and Christianity
are beyond his range of experience. Science, besides being an
instrument for power over nature, is something that makes
you sophisticated enough not to believe in God. Heaven will
be built on earth. Self-salvation, the tragedy of gnosticism
which Nietzsche experienced to the full until it broke his soul,
is a fulfilment of life that will come to every man with the
feeling that he is making his contribution to society according

2. Harold J. Laski, *Faith, Reason and Civilization: An Essay in Historical Analysis*
(New York: Viking Press, 1944), p. 184.

3. *Ibid.*, p. 51.   4. *Ibid.*, p. 143.

to his ability, compensated by a weekly paycheck. There are no problems of human existence in society except the immanent satisfaction of the masses. Political analysis tells you who will be the winner, so that the intellectual can advance in proper time to the position of a court theologian of the Communist empire. And, if you are bright, you will follow him in his expert surf-riding on the wave of the future. The case is too well known today to need further comment. It is the case of the petty paracletes in whom the spirit is stirring, who feel the duty to play a public role and be teachers of mankind, who with good faith substitute their convictions for critical knowledge, and with a perfectly good conscience express their opinions on problems beyond their reach. Moreover, one should not deny the immanent consistency and honesty of this transition from liberalism to communism; if liberalism is understood as the immanent salvation of man and society, communism certainly is its most radical expression; it is an evolution that was already anticipated by John Stuart Mill's faith in the ultimate advent of communism for mankind.

In more technical language one can formulate the problem in the following manner. The three possible varieties of immanentization—teleological, axiological, and activist—are not merely three co-ordinated types but are related to one another dynamically. In every wave of the Gnostic movement the progressivist and utopian varieties will tend to form a political right wing, leaving a good deal of the ultimate perfection to gradual evolution and compromising on a tension between achievement and ideal, while the activist variety will tend to form a political left wing, taking violent action toward the complete realization of the perfect realm. The distribution of the faithful from right to left will in part be determined by such personal equations as enthusiasm, temperament, and consistency; to another, and perhaps the more important part, however, it will be determined by their relation to the civilizational environment in which the Gnostic revolution takes place. For it must never be forgotten that Western society is not all modern but that modernity is a growth within it, in opposition to the classic and Christian tradition. If there were nothing in Western society but gnosticism, the movement toward the left would be irresistible because it lies in the logic of immanentization, and it would have been consummated long ago. In fact, however, the great Western revolutions of the past, after their logical swing to the left, settled down to a public order which reflected the balance of the social forces of the moment, together with their economic interests and civilizational traditions. The apprehension or hope, as the case may be, that the "partial" revolutions of the past will be followed by the "radical" revolution and the establishment of the final realm rests on the assumption that the traditions of Western society are now sufficiently ruined and that the famous masses are ready for the kill.[5]

The dynamics of gnosticism, thus, moves along two lines. In the dimension of historical depth, gnosticism moves from the partial immanentization of the high Middle Ages to the radical immanentization of the present. And with every wave and revolutionary outburst it moves in the amplitude of right and left. The thesis, however, that these two lines of dynamics must now meet according to their inner logic, that Western society is ripe to fall for communism, that the course of Western history is determined by the logic of its modernity and nothing else, is an impertinent piece of Gnostic propaganda at both its silliest and most vicious and certainly has nothing to do with a critical study of politics. Against this thesis must be held a number of facts which today are obscured because the

5. The concepts of "partial" and "radical" revolution were developed by Karl Marx in *Kritik der Hegelschen Rechtsphilosophie*, Einleitung (1843), Vol. I: *Gesamtausgabe*, p. 617.

public debate is dominated by the liberal clichés. In the first place, the Communist movement in Western society itself, wherever it had to rely on its own mass appeal without aid from the Soviet government, has got exactly nowhere at all. The only Gnostic activist movement that achieved a noteworthy measure of success was the National Socialist movement on a limited national basis; and the suicidal nature of such an activist success is amply testified by the atrocious internal corruption of the regime while it lasted as well as by the ruins of the German cities. Second, the present Western plight in the face of the Soviet danger, in so far as it is due to the creation of the previously described power vacuum, is not of Communist making. The power vacuum was created by the Western democratic governments freely, on the height of a military victory, without pressure from anybody. Third, that the Soviet Union is an expanding great power on the Continent has nothing to do with communism. The present extension of the Soviet empire over the satellite nations corresponds substantially to the program of a Slavic empire under Russian hegemony as it was submitted, for instance, by Bakunin to Nicolai I. It is quite conceivable that a non-Communist Russian hegemonic empire would today have the same expanse as the Soviet empire and be a greater danger because it might be better consolidated. Fourth, the Soviet empire, while it is a formidable power, is no danger to Western Europe on the level of material force. Elementary statistics shows that Western manpower, natural resources, and industrial potential are a match to any strength the Soviet empire can muster—not counting our own power in the background. The danger strictly arises from national particularism and the paralyzing intellectual and moral confusion.

The problem of Communist danger, thus, is thrown back on the problem of Western paralysis and self-destructive politics through the Gnostic dream. The previously quoted passages show the source of the trouble. The danger of a sliding from right to left is inherent in the nature of the dream; in so far as communism is a more radical and consistent type of immanentization than progressivism or social utopianism, it has the *logique du cœur* on its side. The Western Gnostic societies are in a state of intellectual and emotional paralysis because no fundamental critique of left-wing gnosticism is possible without blowing up right-wing gnosticism in its course. Such major experiential and intellectual revolutions, however, take their time and the change of at least one generation. One can do no more than formulate the conditions of the problem. There will be a latent Communist danger under the most favorable external circumstances as long as the public debate in Western societies is dominated by the Gnostic clichés. That is to say: as long as the recognition of the structure of reality, the cultivation of the virtues of *sophia* and *prudentia*, the discipline of the intellect, and the development of theoretical culture and the life of the spirit are stigmatized in public as "reactionary," while disregard for the structure of reality, ignorance of facts, fallacious misconstruction and falsification of history, irresponsible opining on the basis of sincere conviction, philosophical illiteracy, spiritual dulness, and agnostic sophistication are considered the virtues of man and their possession opens the road to public success. In brief: as long as civilization is reaction, and moral insanity is progress.

4

The function of gnosticism as the civil theology of Western society, its destruction of the truth of the soul, and its disregard for the problem of existence have been set forth in sufficient detail to make the fatal importance of the problem clear. The inquiry can now return to the great thinker who discovered its nature and tried to solve it by his theory of representation. In the seventeenth century the existence of the

English national society seemed in danger of being destroyed by Gnostic revolutionaries, as today on a larger scale the same danger seems to threaten the existence of Western society as a whole. Hobbes tried to meet the danger by devising a civil theology which made the order of a society in existence the truth which it represented—and by the side of this truth no other should be held. This was an eminently sensible idea in so far as it put the whole weight on existence that had been so badly neglected by the Gnostics. The practical value of the idea, however, rested on the assumption that the transcendent truth which men tried to represent in their societies, after mankind had gone through the experiences of philosophy and Christianity, could be neglected in its turn. Against the Gnostics who did not want society to exist unless its order represented a specific type of truth, Hobbes insisted that any order would do if it secured the existence of society. In order to make this conception valid, he had to create his new idea of man. Human nature would have to find fulfilment in existence itself; a purpose of man beyond existence would have to be denied. Hobbes countered the Gnostic immanentization of the eschaton which endangered existence by a radical immanence of existence which denied the eschaton.

The result of this effort was ambivalent. In order to maintain his position against the fighting churches and sects, Hobbes had to deny that their zeal was inspired, however misguided, by a search for truth. Their struggle had to be interpreted, in terms of immanent existence, as an unfettered expression of their lust for power; and their professed religious concern had to be revealed as a mask for their existential lust. In carrying out this analysis, Hobbes proved to be one of the greatest psychologists of all times; his achievements in unmasking the *libido dominandi* behind the pretense of religious zeal and reforming idealism are as solid today as they were at the time when he wrote. This magnificent psychological achievement, however, was purchased at a heavy price. Hobbes rightly diagnosed the corruptive element of passion in the religiousness of the Puritan Gnostics. He did not, however, interpret passion as the source of corruption in the life of the spirit, but rather the life of the spirit as the extreme of existential passion. Hence, he could not interpret the nature of man from the vantage point of the maximum of differentiation through the experiences of transcendence so that passion, and especially the fundamental passion, *superbia*, could be discerned as the permanently present danger of the fall from true nature; but he had, on the contrary, to interpret the life of passion as the nature of man so that the phenomena of spiritual life appeared as extremes of *superbia*.

According to this conception, the generic nature of man must be studied in terms of human passions; the objects of the passions are no legitimate object of inquiry.[6] This is the fundamental counterposition to classic and Christian moral philosophy. Aristotelian ethics starts from the purposes of action and explores the order of human life in terms of the ordination of all actions toward a highest purpose, the *summum bonum;* Hobbes, on the contrary, insists that there is no *summum bonum*, "as is spoken of in the books of the old moral philosophers."[7] With the *summum bonum*, however, disappears the source of order from human life; and not only from the life of individual man but also from life in society; for, as you will remember, the order of the life in community depends on *homonoia*, in the Aristotelian and Christian sense, that is, on the participation in the common nous. Hobbes, therefore, is faced with the problem of constructing an order of society out of isolated individuals who are not oriented toward a common purpose but only motivated by their individual passions.

The details of the construction are well known. It will be

6. Thomas Hobbes, *Leviathan* (Blackwell ed.), Introduction, p. 6.

7. *Ibid.*, chap. xi, p. 63.

sufficient to recall the main points. Human happiness is for Hobbes a continuous progress of desire from one object to another. The object of man's desire "is not to enjoy once only, and for one instant of time; but to assure for ever, the way of his future desire."[8] "So that in the first place, I put for a general inclination of all mankind, a perpetual and restless desire of power after power, that ceaseth only in death."[9] A multitude of men is not a community but an open field of power drives in competition with each other. The original drive for power, therefore, is aggravated by diffidence of the competitor and by the lust of glorying in successfully outstripping the other man.[10] "This race we must suppose to have no other goal, no other garland, but being foremost." And in this race "continually to be outgone is misery. Continually to outgo the next is felicity. And to forsake the course, is to die."[11] Passion aggravated by comparison is pride.[12] And this pride may assume various forms of which the most important for the analysis of politics was to Hobbes the pride in having divine inspirations, or generally to be in possession of undoubted truth. Such pride in excess is madness.[13] "If some man in Bedlam should entertain you with sober discourse; and you desire in taking leave, to know what he were, that you might another time requite his civility; and he should tell you, he were God the Father; I think you need expect no extravagant action for argument of his madness."[14] If this madness becomes violent and the possessors of the inspiration try to impose it on others, the result in society will be "the seditious roaring of a troubled nation."[15]

8. *Ibid.*   9. *Ibid.*, p. 64.

10. *Ibid.*, chap. xiii, p. 81.

11. Thomas Hobbes, *The Elements of Law, Natural and Politic*, ed. Ferdinand Tönnies (Cambridge, 1928), Part I, chap. ix, Sec. 21.

12. Thomas Hobbes, *Leviathan*, chap. viii, p. 46.

13. *Ibid.*, pp. 46–47.

14. *Ibid.*, pp. 47–48.   15. *Ibid.*, p. 47.

Since Hobbes does not recognize sources of order in the soul, inspiration can be exorcised only by a passion that is even stronger than the pride to be a paraclete, and that is the fear of death. Death is the greatest evil; and if life cannot be ordered through orientation of the soul toward a *summum bonum*, order will have to be motivated by fear of the *summum malum*.[16] Out of mutual fear is born the willingness to submit to government by contract. When the contracting parties agree to have a government, they "confer all their power and strength upon one man, or assembly of men, that may reduce all their wills, by plurality of voices, unto one will."[17]

The acumen of Hobbes shows itself at its best in his understanding that the contractual symbolism which he uses, in accordance with the conventions of the seventeenth century, is not the essence of the matter. The combining into a commonwealth under a sovereign may express itself in legal form, but essentially it is a psychological transformation of the combining persons. The Hobbesian conception of the process in which a political society comes into existence is rather close to Fortescue's conception of the creation of a new *corpus mysticum* through the eruption of a people. The covenanters do not create a government that would represent them as single individuals; in the contracting act they cease to be self-governing persons and merge their power drives into a new person, the commonwealth, and the carrier of this new person, its representative, is the sovereign.

This construction required a few distinctions concerning the meaning of the term "person." "A person, is he, whose words or actions are considered, either as his own, or as representing the words and actions of another man, or of any other thing." When he represents himself, he is a natural person; when he

16. Thomas Hobbes, *De homine*, chap. xi, Art. 6; *De cive*, chap. i, Art. 7. On the problem of fear of death as the *summum malum* see Leo Strauss, *The Political Philosophy of Hobbes* (Oxford, 1934).

17. Thomas Hobbes, *Leviathan*, chap. xvii, p. 112.

represents another, he is called an artificial person. The meaning of person is referred back to the Latin *persona*, and the Greek *prosopon*, as the face, the outward appearance, or the mask of the actor on the stage. "So that a person, is the same that an actor is, both on the stage and in common conversation; and to personate, is to act, or represent himself, or another."[18]

This concept of a person allows Hobbes to separate the visible realm of representative words and deeds from the unseen realm of processes in the soul, with the consequence that the visible words and actions, which always must be those of a definite, physical human being, may represent a unit of psychic processes which arises from the interaction of individual human souls. In the natural condition every man has his own person in the sense that his words and actions represent the power drive of his passions. In the civil condition the human units of passion are broken and fused into a new unit, called the commonwealth. The actions of the single human individuals whose souls have coalesced cannot represent the new person; its bearer is the sovereign. The creation of this person of the commonwealth, Hobbes insists, is "more than consent, or concord," as the language of contract would suggest. The single human persons cease to exist and merge into the one person represented by the sovereign. "This is the generation of that great Leviathan, or rather, to speak more reverently, of that *mortal god*, to which we owe under the *immortal God*, our peace and defence." The covenanting men agree "to submit their wills, every one to his will, and their judgments to his judgment." The fusion of wills is "a real unity of them all"; for the mortal god "hath the use of so much power and strength conferred upon him, that by terror thereof, he is enabled to form the wills of them all, to peace at home, and mutual aid against their enemies abroad."[19]

18. *Ibid.*, chap. xvi, pp. 105 ff.
19. *Ibid.*, chap. xvii, p. 112.

The style of the construction is magnificent. If human nature is assumed to be nothing but passionate existence, devoid of ordering resources of the soul, the horror of annihilation will, indeed, be the overriding passion that compels submission to order. If pride cannot bow to Dike, or be redeemed through grace, it must be broken by the Leviathan who "is king of all the children of pride."[20] If the souls cannot participate in the Logos, then the sovereign who strikes terror into the souls will be "the essence of the commonwealth."[21] The "King of the Proud" must break the *amor sui* that cannot be relieved by the *amor Dei*.[22]

5

Joachim of Flora had created an aggregate of symbols which dominated the self-interpretation of modern political movements in general; Hobbes created a comparable aggregate which expressed the component of radical immanence in modern politics.

The first of these symbols may be called the new psychology. Its nature can be defined best by relating it to the Augustinian psychology from which it derives. St. Augustine distinguished between the *amor sui* and the *amor Dei* as the organizing volitional centers of the soul. Hobbes threw out the *amor Dei* and relied for his psychology on the *amor sui*, in his language the self-conceit or pride of the individual, alone. In this elimination of the *amor Dei* from the interpretation of the psyche a development was consummated that can be traced back at least to the twelfth century. With the appearance of the self-reliant individual on the social scene, the new type and its striving for public success beyond its status attracted attention. In fact, John of Salisbury described it in his *Poli-*

20. *Ibid.*, chap. xxviii, p. 209.
21. *Ibid.*, chap. xvii, p. 112.
22. *Ibid.*, chap. xxviii, p. 209.

craticus in terms closely resembling those of Hobbes.[23] In the wake of the institutional upheavals of the late Middle Ages and the Reformation, then, the type became so common that it appeared as the "normal" type of man and became a matter of general concern. The psychological work of Hobbes was paralleled in his own time by the psychology of Pascal, though Pascal preserved the Christian tradition and described the man who was guided by his passions alone as the man who had fallen a prey to one or the other type of *libido*. And also contemporaneously, with La Rochefoucauld, began the psychology of the man of the "world" who was motivated by his *amour-propre* (the Augustinian *amor sui*). The national ramifications into the French psychology of the *moralistes* and novelists, the English psychology of pleasure-pain, associationism and self-interest, the German enrichments through the psychology of the unconscious of the Romantics and the psychology of Nietzsche, may be recalled in order to suggest the pervasiveness of the phenomenon. A specifically "modern" psychology developed as the empirical psychology of "modern" man, that is, of the man who was intellectually and spiritually disoriented and hence motivated primarily by his

23. John of Salisbury, *Policraticus: Sive De nugis curialium, et vestigiis philosophorum libri octo*, ed. Clement C. J. Webb (Oxford, 1909). The following passages are quoted in the translation of *The Statesman's Book of John of Salisbury*, translated into English with an Introduction by John Dickinson (New York, 1927). Man, ignorant of his true status and the obedience which he owes to God, "aspires to a kind of fictitious liberty, vainly imagining that he can live without fear and can do with impunity whatsoever pleases him, and somehow be straightway like unto God" (viii. 17). "Though it is not given to all men to seize princely or royal power, yet the man who is wholly untainted by tyranny is rare or non-existent. In common speech the tyrant is one who oppresses a whole people by rulership based on force; and yet it is not over a people as a whole that a man can play the tyrant, but he can do so if he will even in the meanest station. For if not over the whole body of the people, still each man will lord it as far as his power extends" (vii. 17). Even the Hobbesian metaphor of the race can be found in John: "And so all contend in the race, and when the goal is reached, that one among them receives the prize who emerges swifter than the rest in the race of ambition, and outruns Peter or any of the disciples of Christ" (vii. 19).

passions. It will be useful to introduce the terms of psychology of orientation and psychology of motivation in order to distinguish a science of the healthy psyche, in the Platonic sense, in which the order of the soul is created by transcendental orientation, from the science of the disoriented psyche which must be ordered by a balance of motivations. "Modern" psychology, in this sense, is an incomplete psychology in so far as it deals only with a certain pneumopathological type of man.

The second symbol concerns the idea of man itself. Since the disoriented type, because of its empirical frequency, was understood as the "normal" type, a philosophical anthropology developed in which the disease was interpreted as the "nature of man." Time does not permit us to enter more deeply into this problem. It must be sufficient to suggest the line which connects contemporary existentialists with the first philosophers of existence in the seventeenth century. What has to be said in criticism of this philosophy of immanent existence was said, on principle, by Plato in his *Gorgias*.

The third symbol, finally, is the specifically Hobbesian creation of the Leviathan. Its significance is hardly understood today because the symbol is smothered under the jargon of absolutism. The preceding account should have made it clear that the Leviathan is the correlate of order to the disorder of Gnostic activists who indulge their *superbia* to the extreme of civil war. The Leviathan cannot be identified with the historical form of absolute monarchy; the royalist contemporaries understood that quite well, and their distrust of Hobbes was amply justified. Nor can the symbol be identified with totalitarianism on its own symbolic level of the final realm of perfection. It rather adumbrates a component in totalitarianism which comes to the fore when a group of Gnostic activists actually achieves the monopoly of existential representation in a historical society. The victorious Gnostics can neither transfigure the nature of man nor establish a terrestrial paradise; what they actually do establish is an omnipotent state which ruthlessly eliminates all sources of resistance and, first of all, the troublesome Gnostics themselves. As far as our experience with totalitarian empires goes, their characteristic feature is the elimination of debate concerning the Gnostic truth which they themselves profess to represent. The National Socialists suppressed the debate of the race question, once they had come to power; the Soviet government prohibits the debate and development of Marxism. The Hobbesian principle that the validity of Scripture derives from governmental sanction and that its public teaching should be supervised by the sovereign is carried out by the Soviet government in the reduction of communism to the "party line." The party line may change, but the change of interpretation is determined by the government. Intellectuals who still insist on having opinions of their own concerning the meaning of the koranic writings are purged. The Gnostic truth that was produced freely by the original Gnostic thinkers is now channeled into the truth of public order in immanent existence. Hence, the Leviathan is the symbol of the fate that actually will befall the Gnostic activists when in their dream they believe they realize the realm of freedom.

6

The symbol of the Leviathan was developed by an English thinker in response to the Puritan danger. Of the major European political societies, however, England has proved herself most resistant against Gnostic totalitarianism; and the same must be said for the America that was founded by the very Puritans who aroused the fears of Hobbes. A word on this question will be in order in conclusion.

The explanation must be sought in the dynamics of gnosticism. You will remember the frequent reminders that modernity is a growth within Western society, in competition with the Mediterranean tradition; and you will, furthermore, remember that gnosticism itself underwent a process of radicalization, from the medieval immanentization of the Spirit that left God in his transcendence to the later radical immanentization of the eschaton as it was to be found in Feuerbach and Marx. The corrosion of Western civilization through gnosticism is a slow process extending over a thousand years. The several Western political societies, now, have a different relation to this slow process according to the time at which their national revolutions occurred. When the revolution occurred early, a less radical wave of gnosticism was its carrier, and the resistance of the forces of tradition was, at the same time, more effective. When the revolution occurred at a later date, a more radical wave was its carrier, and the environment of tradition was already corroded more deeply by the general advance of modernity. The English Revolution, in the seventeenth century, occurred at a time when gnosticism had not yet undergone its radical secularization. You have seen that the left-wing Puritans were eager to present themselves as Christians, though of an especially pure sort. When the adjustments of 1690 were reached, England had preserved the institutional culture of aristocratic parliamentism as well as the mores of a Christian commonwealth, now sanctioned as national institutions. The American Revolution, though its debate was already strongly affected by the psychology of enlightenment, also had the good fortune of coming to its close within the institutional and Christian climate of the *ancien régime*. In the French Revolution, then, the radical wave of gnosticism was so strong that it permanently split the nation into the laicist half that based itself on the Revolution and the conservative half that tried, and tries, to salvage the Christian tradition. The German Revolution, finally, in an environment without strong institutional traditions, brought for the first time into full play economic materialism, racist biology, cor-

rupt psychology, scientism, and technological ruthlessness—
in brief, modernity without restraint. Western society as a
whole, thus, is a deeply stratified civilization in which the
American and English democracies represent the oldest, most
firmly consolidated stratum of civilizational tradition, while
the German area represents its most progressively modern
stratum.

In this situation there is a glimmer of hope, for the American
and English democracies which most solidly in their institutions represent the truth of the soul are, at the same time, existentially the strongest powers. But it will require all our efforts to kindle this glimmer into a flame by repressing Gnostic
corruption and restoring the forces of civilization. At present
the fate is in the balance.

INDEX

✻